# UNDERSTANDING AND APPLYING PRODUCT-PLATFORM STRATEGY

Released August 1, 2016

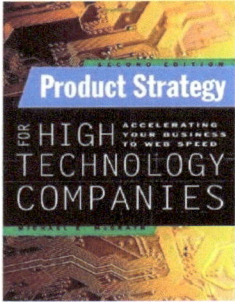

Since 1994 when I first published the concepts of product-platform strategy, *Product Strategy for High Technology Companies* (McGraw Hill, 2001) has become a mainstay of strategy in many industries, particularly for high-technology companies. Some of the most successful companies implemented a product-platform strategy, and many of those who didn't failed as a result. In this new book, as well as others in this series, I expand and update these concepts, adding new lessons learned in the past decade, and illustrate them with current examples.

Since there are several new concepts and so many great examples, I've decided to update *Product Strategy* through a series of new books, each focused on a particular product strategy topic. This first book, *Understanding and Applying Product-Platform Strategy*, starts with the core underlying concepts of platform strategy, based on workshops I have been giving around the world over the last few years.

There are several new concepts that I added or expanded on in this book. The concept of platform layers expands on original concept of elements in complex platforms. As product platforms evolved to be more complex, organizing them into layers became logical.

Platform robustness is introduced to address the issue that not all platforms are created equal, and this builds on the concept of vectors of differentiation in my original book. Competitive advantage can come from having a more robust product-platform strategy than a competitor.

The issues around a platform as part of an ecosystem are now more relevant and discussed in more detail. This has become increasingly important, as more companies have implemented platform strategies that are linked with others.

Also as more companies have leveraged product-platforms into new markets, the concepts of derivative platforms have become more important. So we will examine derivative platforms in more detail.

1

# Michael E. McGrath

Michael McGrath is a successful CEO, management expert, and experienced board member with extensive executive experience in the software industry and technology strategy. He founded and managed PRTM, the most successful management-consulting firm to the high-technology industry; led the successful turnaround of i2 Technologies; is an experienced board director; and is a published expert on strategy and product development.

Michael has been recognized for his expertise in several areas critical to the success of businesses today.

## *Product Strategy*

Michael is a recognized expert in high-technology product strategy. Many successful companies have used the concepts in his book Product Strategy for High-Technology Companies, particularly his strategic concepts on platform strategy, as the basis for product strategy. He continues to actively advise companies on product strategy.

## *Decision Making*

Michael is also a recognized expert in business decision-making. His latest book, Business Decisions, was the culmination of more than 25 years of advising executives throughout the world on business decisions. Michael has appeared as a decision expert for CNBC, CNN International, ABC, and Fox Business; and he has done more than 100 radio interviews on business topics.

## *R&D Management*

He initiated PRTM's product development consulting practice in the late 1980s, creating the PACE® process. PACE has been implemented by more than 1,000 of the largest technology and industrial companies in the world to significantly improve R&D. His books (Next Generation Product Development, and Setting the Pace in Product Development) are standard references for product development. In 2004 he received the first lifetime achievement award from the Product Development and Management Association in recognition of his work in product development and product strategy.

# Contents

# Chapter 1
# Fundamentals of Product-Platform Strategy

Product-platform strategy is the foundation of a strong business strategy, especially in high-technology companies with multiple products based on a common set of shared technologies. Over the last 15-20 years, we have seen companies using a product-platform strategy to outcompete those who had a strategy based primarily on individual products. In *Understanding and Applying Product-Platform Strategy*, we will look at the fundamentals of platform strategy, the characteristics that make it successful, how to manage it, and how to use it to drive rapid growth.

As was the approach with previous *Product Strategy* books, we will focus on examples not only to illustrate the strategy, but in fact, as the basis for deriving the concepts behind product-platform strategy. A number of different examples will be used to illustrate the concepts, but a few, particularly Apple, will be used as examples to illustrate concepts throughout the book.

To start off, the best way to consider product-platform strategy is as a definition for strategic thinking, planning, and decision-making. This forces a company to separate product-platform strategy from its strategy for product-lines and individual products, enabling it to concentrate on the most important strategic issues. It can leverage platform technologies across a broad range of products, while also providing operational leverage from commonality. Finally, a robust product-platform strategy provides a powerful growth engine by enabling a company to leverage a platform into new markets.

A product platform is a common foundation of shared elements such as technologies, especially the defining technology, implemented across a range of products. These shared elements are not necessarily complete in the sense that they are something that could be sold to a customer, although we will see a few examples of this. These shared elements are leveraged to create products through the product platform.

Let's start off with some general characteristics and important product platform definitions:

- **Layers** - Generally a product platform has multiple layers, which are essentially categories of similar elements such as common software elements, common hardware components, business process, services, etc. These layers are combined to build the platform. This expands on the concept of layers of elements from my previous writing on platform strategy, and is helpful as platforms became more complex.
- **Elements** – These are the individual components in a platform layer such as specific technologies, software applications or functions, business process elements, etc. In a successful platform strategy, these elements are improved continuously and new elements are added to each layer.
- **Defining technology** – This is the most critical platform layer. It defines the platform's capabilities and limitations, and usually the competitive advantage of all products created from the plat-

5

form. It is literally what defines the platform, and the platform lifecycle is usually determined by the competitiveness of the defining technology.

- **Supporting layers/elements** – These are the other layers and elements within a layer in the platform that are necessary to complete the platform. These may also be unique and provide competitive advantage, but they tend to be similar to those used by competitors.
- **Segmenting layers/elements** – As multiple product lines are deployed from a common platform, segmenting layers and elements of the platform essentially create these differing product lines.
- **Derivative platform** – In some cases, a derivative platform is created to enter a new market. Typically, a derivative platform incorporates one or more new platform layers while leveraging some of the critical layers/elements, typically the defining technology, from a common platform that underlies multiple derivative platforms. Derivative platforms are also something emphasized more with an increasing number of successful examples.
- **Individual products** – These are the specific products created from the common underlying product platform, which are sold to customers. Products are revenue generating. Products may sometimes be grouped into product lines.

As one would expect, product platforms vary widely across industries. Amazon's product platform consists of its software foundation for browsing, searching, and reviewing content as well as the evaluation tools such as rankings and customer reviews, combined with its order processing, fulfillment and supply-chain capabilities. Netflix platform includes its video streaming capabilities, video content, and its user interface. BMW views its platform as common modules such as the powertrain, driving dynamics, electronics, and body and interior trim that it applies across multiple product-lines (series) of cars. Tesla has a unique platform based on its proprietary powertrain and unique approach to using electric batteries. Keurig has a unique platform for its single-serving coffee brewing and k-cups. We will review these and other examples in more detail, but first let's start out with what is perhaps the most successful company ever built upon product-platform strategy: Apple

## APPLE'S PLATFORM

Apple has been perhaps the most successful company in history, and its success is based on an exceptional product-platform strategy. Over the decade from 2004 to 2014, Apple grew from $10 billion in revenue to $182 billion. Its market value is more than $800 billion.

Apple's product platform strategy began when Steve Jobs' articulated his vision for the future Apple platform of a Digital Hub on January 9, 2001. At that time, he introduced several software applications for this Digital Hub platform, including iTunes, which was going to become the first layer of this new product platform. The iPod fol-

| Apple Stock Price Increase | |
|---|---|
| Dec. 2000 | $1.00 |
| June 2015 | $128.88 |
| Return | 12888% |

lowed later that year in October and then the iTunes store in April 2003, setting the stage for the iPhone on January 9, 2007. The Apps store was introduced in 2008, creating another platform layer and new derivative platform, the iPad, was released on January 27, 2010, along with iBooks and the iBookstore.

6

Apple continued extending and leveraging its platform with Apple Pay, the Apple Watch, Apple TV, and Apple Music.

It's clear that Apples success and growth was based on an exceptional platform strategy. Since Steve launched Apple's new platform vision in January 2001, Apple has been extraordinarily successful. Its stock price has increased from a split adjusted $1 to more than $100 per share. If you understood Steve's platform vision that he articulated that day and had faith in his creative ability to build this platform, you could have made a great investment. A $10,000 investment in Apple prior to the launch of its new platform vision would have turned into $1.3 million 15 years later.[1]

This is a incredible story based on a truly remarkable platform strategy, so let's look more closely at Apple product platform that is illustrated for the Apple iPhone. We will look at how this basic platform is leveraged into similar derivative platforms later on.

The best way to view the Apple product platform is as multiple layers, containing numerous elements within each layer.

**iOS Software Layer**

Let's examine each of these layers in Apple's platform, starting with the iOS Software Layer, positioned just below the iPhone Hardware Layer. This is the defining technology of the platform. It includes basic software functionality for the user interface, direct manipulation, multi-touch gestures, rotation, etc. In addition, it includes the cellular software that supports a very large number of cellular services worldwide. Then there are basic support functions such as the home screen functionality, notifications center, multi-tasking, photo support, utilities, etc. The Siri voice command capability was introduced in 2012. Apple is continually expanding and improving the iOS software layer of its platform with annual improvements, and most of the functionality is used across all of the iPhone product lines and derivative platforms such as the iPad and Apple Watch. This iOS software layer provides the basic user interface and defines how customers use the iPhone and other derivative products.

**iPhone Hardware**

| Touch Screen | Simple Design | Camera | Display | Power | Processor & Memory | Graphics | Cellular Connectivity | Sensors | Sim Card |
|---|---|---|---|---|---|---|---|---|---|

**Software iOS**

| User Interface | Direct Manipulation | Multi-Touch Gestures | Rotation | Wi-Fi | Cellular | Home Screen | Folders | Notification Center | Multi Tasking | Utilities | Siri |
|---|---|---|---|---|---|---|---|---|---|---|---|

**Included Applications**

| Phone | Mail | Browser (Safari) | Music Player | Maps | Video Player | Text Mess | Cal | Notifi-cations | Photo Viewer | Face Time | Photo Booth | Stocks | Weath- | Notes | News stand | Re-minder | Voice Memos | Calc | Cont | Comp. | Game Center | Pass book |
|---|---|---|---|---|---|---|---|---|---|---|---|---|---|---|---|---|---|---|---|---|---|---|

**Media Management**

| Media Player | CD Ripper | Digital Asset Mgmt. | Playlists | Pod Casting | Tag Editor | Cover Flow | Music Metadata | Genius Playlist | Library Sharing | Party Shuffle | Video player | iTunes Match | iTunes Cloud | iTunes Radio | iPhone Activation | Device Synchr. |
|---|---|---|---|---|---|---|---|---|---|---|---|---|---|---|---|---|

**Content (iTunes Store)**

| Music | Movies | TV Shows | Books | Audio Books | Podcasts | Newspapers | Magazines | iTunes University | iPod Games |
|---|---|---|---|---|---|---|---|---|---|

**Apps (App Store)**

| Games | New stand | Busin. | Catalog | Educa-tion | Entertain-ment | Finance | Food & Drink | Health & Fitness | Lifestyle | Medical | Music | Naviga-tion | News | Photo & Video | Product. | Ref. | Sports | Travel | Utilities | Weather |
|---|---|---|---|---|---|---|---|---|---|---|---|---|---|---|---|---|---|---|---|---|

## Included Applications Layer

The next layer is the Included Applications Layer. These are the applications that Apple includes for free, such as phone capabilities, email, browser, music player, maps, video player, text messaging, photo viewer, stocks, weather, notes, reminders, news stand, calculator, game center, passbook, and many more. Here again, Apple is continually extending these, recently Apple Pay was added, as well as the Health Center. These included applications provide additional value to customers by making the iPhone more functional. By extending and adding to these each year, Apple makes the iPhone and related products increasingly valuable, supporting its higher price and increasing its vector of differentiation, as we will discuss later.

## Media Management Layer (iTunes)

Media management is done through the Apple iTunes application layer, which was the first part of the platform released on January 9, 2001 as the starting point for Steve Jobs' Digital Hub vision. iTunes is a media player, which plays, downloads, and organizes digital music and video files on a computer and subsequently manages these for a range of mobile devices. In its first version, the focus of iTunes was primarily on enabling the user to digitize CDs for use on computers or an iPod. Since then this media management layer has increasingly added new capabilities and expanded beyond music.

## Content Layer (iTunes Store)

The content layer (essentially the iTunes store) includes a broad range of content, in various media formats, such as music, movies, TV shows, books, audio books, podcasts, newspapers, magazines, etc. Content is an essential layer of the platform because it is what the user actually consumes. Apple splits content revenue with the content providers, generally taking 30% of the revenue, and manages the distribution of the content. The value of the content helps to enhance the value of the platform and also generates substantial revenue. In 2015, Apple earned almost $20 billion on service revenue, mostly content and Apps. This business along would be one of the 200 largest companies in the world, demonstrating how a platform layer can also be a revenue-generating product.

## Apps (App Store)

The Apps layer of the platform was added July 10, 2008 when Apple opened the Apps store and enabled third party developers to run applications on the iPhone. This was a controversial platform addition, which Steve Jobs originally fought against, but it has proven to be successful. As of early 2015, Apple had more than 1.5 million apps with more than 50 billion downloads.

## iPhone Hardware Layer

The final layer is the segmenting layer for the iPhone, which is the hardware layer. The iPhone was first introduced January 9, 2007 and has since gone through ten generational changes through 2015 – one every year! The iPhone hardware layer is quite complex, including the touch screen (which debuted with the phone's introduction), camera, power, processor and memory, graphics engine, cellular connectivity, sensors, etc. The hardware layer is different with different product lines, such as the iPad, and we will look at these derivative platforms later.

8

Apple built this platform pictured in the figure over time, starting in 2001, adding new layers and leveraging the platform across several derivative platforms, including iPods, iPhones, iPads, Apple TV and the Apple watch. Every year it releases improvements to each layer of the platform, extending its competitive advantage.

## AMAZON'S PLATFORM

Amazon was launched in 1996 based on an ambitious platform strategy. Jeff Bezos did not just create an online bookstore, he pioneered a revolutionary product platform for retail sales. From this common platform, Amazon launched an incredible number of "stores" or product categories – everything from books, to toys, to consumer electronics, to jewelry, and many many more. We will look more closely at this when we discuss creating new product lines from a platform. Amazon went public in 1997, soon after launching the company. In the 18

| Amazon Stock Price Increase | |
|---|---|
| May 1997 | $1.50 |
| June 2015 | $430.77 |
| Return | 28718% |

years since, the stock has appreciated from $1.50 to more than $430 per share. If you invested $10,000 in its IPO, you would have made $2.8 million.[2]

Right from the beginning Amazon's strategy was to create a robust platform, beyond selling books online. In fact, if it's strategy was a single product, an online bookstore, it could have done this much easier. The Amazon product platform consists of five primary layers, as illustrated. The top layer provides software for browsing, searching, and reviewing content. This enables a user to search for a product by title or description, or browse selections by category or key word. It then presents the content in a useful way to aid in making a purchase decision. First introduced for books, these capabilities were later leveraged to all other product lines.

The next layer provides evaluation tools to help customers make purchase decisions. These tools include rankings, customer reviews, similar purchases, etc. These tools are based on an increasingly large database that enable customers to make more informed decisions than ever before, giving Amazon an increasing large advantage over competitors.

The third layer is the software for availability checking, order processing, and order tracking, including its patented one-click buying innovation. These are again leveraged across a wide variety of products (stores).

Behind all of this is another layer, its complex operations for order fulfillment and its supply chain, which is both enormous and efficient. This includes is physical distribution and warehousing strategy, which has evolved significantly as it expanded into new product lines.

The final layer underlying all of this is a very heavy IT infrastructure that operates all of its applications. Much of this infrastructure was later leveraged into a new very successful commercial enterprise, further fueling Amazon's growth.

## KEURIG'S PLATFORM

In 1996 Green Mountain Coffee Roasters (GMCR) invested in Keurig, buying a 35% interest in the company. Keurig's first brewer, the B2000, was made for office use and launched in 1998. K-Cup packs with tea were introduced in 2000, followed by other beverages. By 2003, there were more than 40,000 commercial brewers in American offices. Also in 2003, GMCR increased its ownership percentage to 43%. The company's B100 home brewer was introduced in 2004, and the company began looking at going public. In 2006, GMCR acquired Keurig for $160 million, and Keurig is now a wholly owned subsidiary of GMCR.

In 2012, the Keurig Vue brewing system was introduced, in order to increase the choices users have in brewing beverages. In 2012, a commercial version of the Keurig Vue brewer was offered, which allows choice of temperature, cup size, and brew strength. Keurig also released the Rivo brewing system, the first single-cup espresso system, which can froth fresh milk for lattes or cappuccinos. In 2014 GMCR became Keurig Green Mountain (KGM) by shareholder vote.

From 2008 to 2011, Keurig's revenue increased 8X on the growth of the Keurig single-cup coffee makers. The success of this new platform was incredible, with many brewer variations based on the common platform and a large royalty stream from k-cups. Its stock price increased from $0.26 in January 1999 when the Keurig system began penetrating the market to $151 per share in October 2014. However, when Keurig introduced the 2.0

| Keurig Stock Price Increase | |
|---|---|
| Jan 1999 | $0.26 |
| Oct. 2014 | $151.00 |
| Return | 58077% |

brewers in September of 2014, it landed with a thud. The public was disenchanted with the 2.0's new technology to lock out "unauthorized" single-serve coffee pods — in other words, pods from companies without a licensing deal with Keurig. This caused its stock price to slide dramatically (in part because this company has always been a target for short sellers). Recently the company tried to correct the problem by opening its new system to others. We will discuss this more in the Platform Ecosystem chapter.

The K-Cup platform is designed to brew a single cup of coffee, tea, hot chocolate, or other hot beverage. The coffee grounds are in a single serving unit, called a "K-Cup". The single-cup brewing platform pierces the foil seal on top of the plastic K-Cup pack with a spray nozzle, while piercing the bottom of the K-Cup pack with a discharge nozzle. Grounds contained inside the K-Cup pack are in a paper filter. Hot water is forced through the K-Cup pack, passing through the grounds and through the filter. A brewing temperature of 192 degrees Fahrenheit (89 Celsius) is the default setting, with some models permitting users to adjust the temperature. The original patents expired in 2012, but Keurig has some later patents on the filters used in the K-Cups.

10

Keurig sells many models based on this platform for use with K-Cup packs, for household and commercial use. Keurig also sells brewers that use new Vue Packs instead of K-Cup Packs. The Vue system offers more control of the brew with a wider range of mug sizes. Unlike K-Cups, Vue Packs can be emptied and recycled after use. Some models can read the RFID tags embedded in Vue packs to select the optimal brew settings for each variety of beverage automatically and brew coffee at different strengths. K-Cup packs come in wide range of choices. Green Mountain Coffee Roasters owns and licenses many beverage brands, offering hundreds flavors. Some of the flavors include tea, hot chocolate, lemonades and cider and other fruit flavors.

In September 2015, Keurig launched Keurig Kold, an entirely different platform which created a variety of cold beverages including soft drinks, functional beverages, and sparkling waters. The machine brewed beverages from The Coca-Cola Company and the Dr. Pepper Snapple Group, in addition to Keurig's own line of flavored sparkling and non-sparkling waters and teas, sports drinks, and soda-fountain drinks. This new platform proved to be a failure because it was too bulky and too expensive (both the machine and the pods). Keurig recalled the Kold in early 2016. On December 7, 2015, an investor group acquired Keurig Green Mountain for $13.9 billion.

## NATIONAL INSTRUMENTS PLATFORM

National Instruments disrupted the traditional test and measurement market by using a common platform, driven by software, to replace individual test and measurement equipment. Perhaps this is best described by a Stephens Inc. report on the company May 14, 2015.[3]

*NATI presents a unique platform and "ecosystem" in both Test & Measurement (T&M) and Embedded Monitoring & Control. The core of National Instrument's (NATI) offering is its Labview graphical programming platform, and accompanying user/developer ecosystem and "app store." This platform approach provides NATI an opportunity to further disrupt the traditional T&M space and take advantage of secular growth within the Embedded space driven by the Industrial Internet of Things theme. NATI targets both the Test & Measurement and Embedded Monitoring & Control markets with a common set of hardware and software offerings:*

- *Test & Measurement. Utilizing a modular approach anchored by NATI's Labview software platform, Scientists & Engineers are able to design tests of physical phenomena for products/devices with applicability throughout the development cycle from prototyping to production.*
- *Embedded Monitoring & Control. This represents a newer opportunity for NATI as companies now focus more on automation / monitoring devices in the field. Utilizing the same Labview design platform as on the T&M side, Engineers are able to design a computer module (brain) that allows a device/machine to interact with the physical world, either by automating a motion or monitoring its current status.*

*We see NATI's disruptive platform offering of hardware supported by the Company's Labview software and accompanying "ecosystem" as a unique competitive advantage. The differentiation lies in NATI's*

11

*Labview software platform, which integrates the Company's various hardware offerings by allowing* Scientists/Engineers an easy, *re-configurable platform for designing T&M and Embedded systems.*

From a similar report on the company from Oppenheimer & Co on July 30, 2015[4].

*Its approach is also modular (multiple instruments in a single box), in contrast to the industry standard box instrument design (stand-alone instruments). NI's products have three basic components, software, hardware, and modules.*

*LabVIEW is graphics-based (versus text-based) application software introduced in 1986 to connect instruments to the devices. National Instruments wanted to create an intuitive, easy to use software product that was more of a functional general-purpose language than a domain-specific language. That said, it has succeeded in creating a language that is easy to use by engineers and scientists in the applications of T&M, data acquisition, and control. Indeed, it has amassed perhaps an 80% share of the application software market for the T&M domain.*

*CompactDAQ is similar to PXI in that it is a modular chassis with the flexibility for up to eight modules in one device and interfaces with LabVIEW. However, DAQ has a smaller footprint, is less sensitive but more durable and suited for difficult environments. It is controlled via a USB connection to a computer. It has ~95 modules and tends to be most effective for general purpose test in lower volume applications and data acquisition.*

*CompactRIO has a similar footprint to DAQ and shares its ~95 modules. However, it has an embedded controller and is designed with an FPGA chip that allows the device to be reprogrammed at will and untethers it from an external computer. The result is a machine that is very fast with excellent sensitivity. Typically, RIO is sold in volumes to OEMs who build it in and embed it into their machinery. As such, it is good for acquiring data and controlling machinery, and when connected to plant-level controls can be an important element of the IIoT (industrial internet of things).*

National Instruments started developing this platform from almost its founding and went public in 1995. In the early 2000s, it began to expand its platform strategy, creating many new products from a common platform, and today the company has a common platform with a few variations for different markets and hundreds of products. If you look at its stock price, it has increased from $8.47 in January 1999 to $31.08 in June 2015.

## ALARM.COM'S PLATFROM

Alarm.com is a leading platform solution for the connected home, transforming the market from what previously was primarily point-solutions. Through cloud-based services, Alarm.com makes connected home technology broadly accessible to millions of home and business owners. A multi-tenant software-as-a-service, or SaaS, platform enables home and business owners to intelligently secure their properties and automate and control a broad array of connected devices through a single, intuitive user interface. Its connected home platform currently has more than 2.3 million residential and business subscribers and connects to more than 25 million devices.

Alarm.com solutions connect people in new ways with their properties and devices, making them safer, smarter and more efficient. Its scalable, flexible platform is designed to meet a wide range of user needs with its breadth of services, depth of feature capability and broad support for the growing Internet of Things devices in the home. There are currently four offerings from that platform, which can be used individually or combined and integrated within a single user interface accessible through the web and mobile apps:

- *Interactive Security.* Always-on intelligent security and awareness solution that operates through a dedicated, cellular connection to provide safe, reliable protection and withstand common vulnerabilities like line cuts, power outages and network connectivity issues. The solution includes a powerful mobile app, anytime alerts and customized triggers, and provides 24x7 emergency response through integrated service providers.
- *Intelligent Automation.* Integrated home automation solution that allows users to easily and remotely connect and control devices and systems such as security systems, garage doors, lights, door locks, thermostats, electrical appliances, environmental sensors and other connected devices. The cloud-based platform uses data and sophisticated algorithms to learn activity patterns and recommend intelligent optimizations.
- *Video Monitoring.* Video-as-a-service solution delivering on-demand viewing, cloud-based video storage and intelligently triggered recording with anytime access. The comprehensive suite of video services includes live streaming, smart clip capture, high-definition continuous recording and instant video alerts delivered to users through the web and mobile apps.
- *Energy Management.* Comprehensive energy monitoring and management solution for controlling energy consumption and comfort. Web and mobile apps integrate with connected thermostats, power meters, lights, shades, solar panels and appliances to control devices and manage temperature as well as provide real-time insights into home energy usage and efficiency. The intelligent platform delivers activity-based learning optimization as well as location-based adjustments for effortless energy management.

The Alarm.com platform is based on several emerging technologies: mobile devices, cloud infrastructure, and the Internet of Things. Existing and legacy approaches to home automation are point products not platforms. Home control products are highly fragmented and made up of multiple disparate devices which provide only a single function, requiring the user to manage multiple, disconnected user interfaces. Often these products do not provide a way for service provider to remotely service their customers. They tend to be closed ecosystems and do not scale to support the expanding Internet of Things. These systems limit the ability of a consumer to add new devices, as they are restricted to a small set of compatible options. The devices lack sufficient intelligence. These products are only able to respond to direct commands and are not able to act independently on the user's behalf based on activity happening in and around the home. Finally, since most legacy products are not cloud-based, they cannot receive automatic updates of new software, and risk becoming obsolete. Alarm.com's revenue increased from $96 million in 2012 to $167 million in 2014. The company went public in June 2015.

13

Lego is a well-known company built upon a platform strategy, literally brick by brick. Over the last 10-15 years, Lego leveraged this platform into a wide range of products, growing much faster than competitors to build the second largest toy company in the world. The fascinating part of the Lego story is that it adopted a platform strategy from what would have been just a single product, Lego bricks, with limited business potential. Instead it saw beyond the single product and envisioned that the bricks could be used to create a wide variety of building sets and kits. Today there are more than 1,000 different Lego building sets and kits available. Target alone carries more than 900 of them.

The Lego Group was founded by Ole Kirk Christiansen, a carpenter from Denmark, who began making wooden toys in 1932. In 1947, Lego expanded to begin producing plastic toys. In 1949 Lego began producing, among other new products, an early version of the now familiar interlocking bricks, calling them "Automatic Binding Bricks". By 1951 plastic toys accounted for half of the Lego Company's output, even though the Danish many people felt that plastic would never be able to replace traditional wooden toys. Although a common sentiment, Lego toys seem to have become a significant exception to the dislike of plastic in children's toys, due in part to the high standards set by Ole Kirk.

**Lego sales growth has outpaced that of Mattel, Hasbro**
In billions

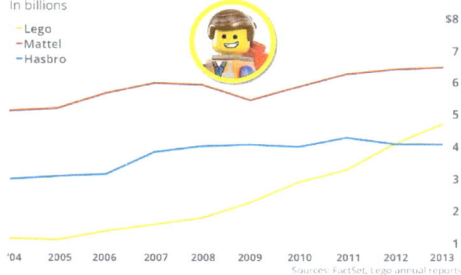

- Lego
- Mattel
- Hasbro

$8
7
6
5
4
3
2
1

'04  2005  2006  2007  2008  2009  2010  2011  2012  2013
Sources: FactSet, Lego annual reports

By 1954, Christiansen's son, Godtfred, saw the immense potential in Lego bricks to become a system for creative play, but the bricks still had some problems from a technical standpoint: their locking ability was limited and they were not versatile. In 1958, the modern brick design was developed; however, it took another five years to find the right material for it, ABS (acrylonitrile butadiene styrene) polymer. The modern Lego brick design was patented in 1958. The Lego Group's Duplo product line was introduced in 1969. It is a range of simple blocks which measure twice the width, height and depth of standard Lego blocks for younger children. In 1978, Lego produced the first mini-figures, which have since become a staple in most sets

The Lego product platform is based on its original brick technology, a wide variety but consistent set of bricks, and its design and manufacturing skills. Lego pieces of all varieties constitute a universal system. Despite variation in the design and the purposes of individual pieces over the years, each piece remains compatible in some way with existing pieces. Lego bricks from 1958 still interlock with those made now, and Lego sets for young children are compatible with those made for teenagers. According to Wikipedia, six pieces of 2x4 bricks can be combined in 915,103,765 ways.

Each Lego piece must be manufactured to an exacting degree of precision. When two pieces are engaged they must fit firmly, yet be easily disassembled. The machines that manufacture Lego bricks have tolerances as small as 10 micrometers. This is a critical part of Lego's defining technology.

14

Since the 1950s, the Lego Group has released thousands of sets with a variety of themes, including space, robots, pirates, trains, Vikings, castle, dinosaurs, undersea exploration, and wild west. Some of the classic themes that continue to the present day include Lego City (a line of sets depicting city life introduced in 1973) and Lego Technic (a line with more unique pieces; rotating gears introduced in 1977).

Over the years, Lego has licensed themes from numerous cartoon and film franchises and even some from video games. These include *Batman*, *Indiana Jones*, *Star Wars*, and *Minecraft*. Lego has also initiated a platform extension, the robotics line of toys called 'Mindstorms' in 1999, and has continued to expand and update this range ever since. The roots of the product originate from a programmable brick developed at the MIT Media Lab. The programmable Lego brick which is at the heart of these robotics sets has undergone several updates and redesigns, with the latest being called the 'EV3' brick, being sold under the name of Lego Mindstorms EV3. The set includes sensors that detect touch, light, sound and ultrasonic waves, with several others being sold separately, including an RFID reader.

Lego also used its brand to diversify into businesses not directly related to its platform, including: six Legoland amusement parks (70% ownership was sold in 2005), 125 retail stores, a business consultancy for creative thinking that uses Lego blocks, video games, board games, and films/TV. Some of these were not as successful as hoped and drained company resources.

15

Pixar is constantly producing animated movies from its powerful development platform. For over 25 years, Pixar, which is now owned by The Walt Disney Company, has used an image processing technology called RenderMan that converts two-dimensional images into three-dimensional graphics. It's the core (defining) technology that gives depth to flat images by adding more color and shading. Pixar continuously upgrades this technology to make it easier for animators to do their job. For example, one major development is a new feature that automatically adds lighting around objects in a scene so that animators don't have to — even after the finalized scene is already completed.

This was seen in Pixar's movie Inside Out, where an ever-present glow continuously emanates from the character, Joy. Joy is essentially a source of light in the movie that literally lights up characters and objects as if she were a lamp. The light that radiates from her body must spill onto other objects in a realistic way. Using the upgraded rendering software, animators didn't have to manually insert lighting to each scene when Joy is on-screen. Instead, the software automatically added light to her along with illuminating background scenery and her companions.

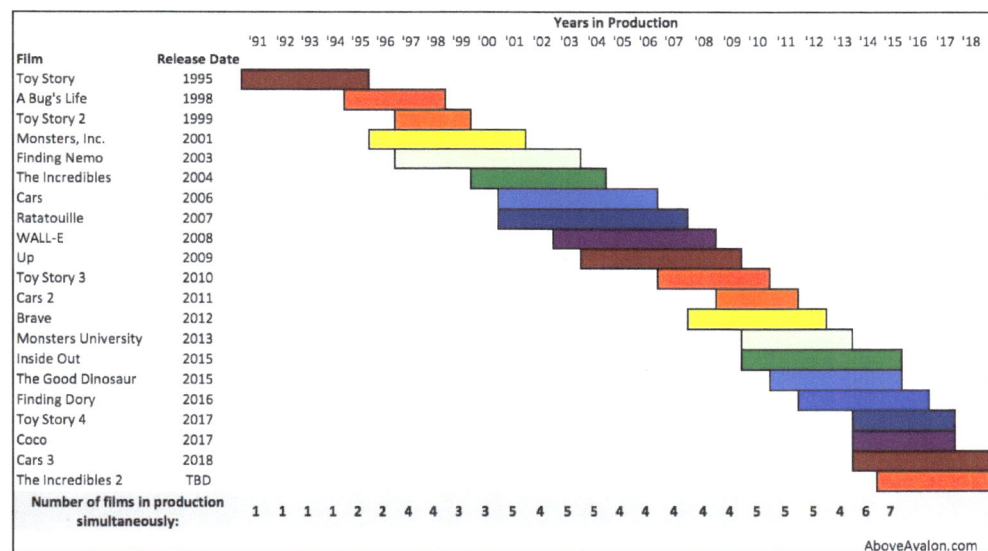

**Years in Production**

| Film | Release Date | '91 | '92 | '93 | '94 | '95 | '96 | '97 | '98 | '99 | '00 | '01 | '02 | '03 | '04 | '05 | '06 | '07 | '08 | '09 | '10 | '11 | '12 | '13 | '14 | '15 | '16 | '17 | '18 |
|---|---|---|---|---|---|---|---|---|---|---|---|---|---|---|---|---|---|---|---|---|---|---|---|---|---|---|---|---|---|
| Toy Story | 1995 | | | | | | | | | | | | | | | | | | | | | | | | | | | | |
| A Bug's Life | 1998 | | | | | | | | | | | | | | | | | | | | | | | | | | | | |
| Toy Story 2 | 1999 | | | | | | | | | | | | | | | | | | | | | | | | | | | | |
| Monsters, Inc. | 2001 | | | | | | | | | | | | | | | | | | | | | | | | | | | | |
| Finding Nemo | 2003 | | | | | | | | | | | | | | | | | | | | | | | | | | | | |
| The Incredibles | 2004 | | | | | | | | | | | | | | | | | | | | | | | | | | | | |
| Cars | 2006 | | | | | | | | | | | | | | | | | | | | | | | | | | | | |
| Ratatouille | 2007 | | | | | | | | | | | | | | | | | | | | | | | | | | | | |
| WALL-E | 2008 | | | | | | | | | | | | | | | | | | | | | | | | | | | | |
| Up | 2009 | | | | | | | | | | | | | | | | | | | | | | | | | | | | |
| Toy Story 3 | 2010 | | | | | | | | | | | | | | | | | | | | | | | | | | | | |
| Cars 2 | 2011 | | | | | | | | | | | | | | | | | | | | | | | | | | | | |
| Brave | 2012 | | | | | | | | | | | | | | | | | | | | | | | | | | | | |
| Monsters University | 2013 | | | | | | | | | | | | | | | | | | | | | | | | | | | | |
| Inside Out | 2015 | | | | | | | | | | | | | | | | | | | | | | | | | | | | |
| The Good Dinosaur | 2015 | | | | | | | | | | | | | | | | | | | | | | | | | | | | |
| Finding Dory | 2016 | | | | | | | | | | | | | | | | | | | | | | | | | | | | |
| Toy Story 4 | 2017 | | | | | | | | | | | | | | | | | | | | | | | | | | | | |
| Coco | 2017 | | | | | | | | | | | | | | | | | | | | | | | | | | | | |
| Cars 3 | 2018 | | | | | | | | | | | | | | | | | | | | | | | | | | | | |
| The Incredibles 2 | TBD | | | | | | | | | | | | | | | | | | | | | | | | | | | | |
| **Number of films in production simultaneously:** | | | | | | 1 | 1 | 1 | 1 | 2 | 2 | 4 | 4 | 3 | 3 | 5 | 4 | 5 | 5 | 4 | 4 | 4 | 4 | 5 | 5 | 5 | 4 | 6 | 7 |

AboveAvalon.com

The efficiency gains that come from leveraging a constantly improving platform can be seen in the chart showing the number of films that can be in production at the same time, the increasing number of films that can be released each year, and the shortening of development lifecycles at the same time.

With all the advancements in technology and better graphics, Pixar has also had to improve its computing power to accommodate resource-heavy software. The company maintains a vast data center known as a render farm that's filled with thousands of servers, storage hardware, and other gear needed to bring its animated movies to life. It took around 3,000 processors to render the movies The Incredibles and Cars, two films from the mid 2000s. For more recent films like Monsters University and Inside Out, that number has soared to around 20,000 processors. This vast computing power is another layer of Pixar's product-platform.[5]

## WALT DISNEY PLATFORM STRATEGY

Walt Disney is a large diversified company based on a platform strategy. Actually Walt Disney was one of the early visionaries of platform strategy. As you can see in this drawing he did in 1957, he envisioned the platform leverage of a creative talent layer creating theatrical films with the characters and stories leveraged into TV, merchandising, music, publications and then theme parks, starting with Disneyland.

17

Today that original platform has been leveraged into a substantial derivative platform of parks and resorts, with each location in turn creating a new geographical platform for many additional revenue sources. The Company owns and operates the Walt Disney World Resort in Florida; the Disneyland Resort in California; a Disney Resort & Spa in Hawaii; the Disney Vacation Club; the Disney Cruise Line; and Adventures by Disney. The Company manages and has effective ownership interests of 81% in Disneyland Paris, 47% in Hong Kong Disneyland Resort and 43% in Shanghai Disney Resort. The Company also licenses our intellectual property to a third party for the operations of the Tokyo Disney Resort in Japan.

The Company's Walt Disney Imagineering unit is a platform layer that designs and develops new theme park concepts and attractions as well as resort properties.

The businesses in the Parks and Resorts segment generate revenues from the sale of admissions to theme parks, sales of food, beverage and merchandise, charges for room nights at hotels, sales of cruise and other vacation packages and sales and rentals of vacation club properties.

**Walt Disney World Resort**

The Walt Disney World Resort is located 22 miles southwest of Orlando, Florida, on approximately 25,000 acres of land.

The resort includes theme parks (the Magic Kingdom, Epcot, Disney's Hollywood Studios and Disney's Animal Kingdom); hotels; vacation club properties; a retail, dining and entertainment complex; a sports complex; conference centers; campgrounds; golf courses; water parks; and other recreational facilities designed to attract visitors for an extended stay. The Walt Disney World Resort is marketed through a variety of international, national and local advertising and promotional activities. A number of attractions and restaurants in each of the theme parks are sponsored by other corporations through long-term agreements.

- *Magic Kingdom* — The Magic Kingdom consists of six themed areas: Adventureland, Fantasyland, Frontierland, Liberty Square, Main Street USA and Tomorrowland. Each land provides a unique guest experience featuring themed attractions, live Disney character interactions, restaurants. Additionally, there are daily parades and a nighttime fireworks extravaganza, *Wishes*.
- *Epcot* — Epcot consists of two major themed areas: Future World and World Showcase. Future World dramatizes certain historical developments and addresses the challenges facing the world today through pavilions devoted to showcasing science and technology innovations, communication, energy, transportation, use of imagination, nature and food production, the ocean environment and space. World Showcase presents a community of nations focusing on the culture, traditions and accomplishments of people around the world. Countries represented with pavilions include Canada, China, France, Germany, Italy, Japan, Mexico, Morocco, Norway, the United Kingdom and the United States. Both areas feature themed attractions, restaurants and merchandise shops. Epcot also features *Illuminations: Reflections of Earth*, a nighttime entertainment spectacular.
- *Disney's Hollywood Studios* — Disney's Hollywood Studios consists of eight themed areas: Animation Courtyard, Commissary Lane, Echo Lake, Hollywood Boulevard, Mickey Avenue, Pixar Place, Streets of America and Sunset Boulevard. The eight areas provide behind-the-scenes

18

glimpses of Hollywood-style action through various shows and attractions and offer themed food service and merchandise facilities. The park also features *Fantasmic!*, a nighttime entertainment spectacular. In August 2015, the Company announced two new themed lands coming to the park based on the Star Wars and Toy Story franchises.

- ***Disney's Animal Kingdom*** — Disney's Animal Kingdom consists of a 145-foot tall Tree of Life centerpiece surrounded by six themed areas: Africa, Asia, Dinoland U.S.A., Discovery Island, Oasis and Rafiki's Planet Watch. Each themed area contains attractions, entertainment, restaurants and merchandise shops. The park features more than 300 species of mammals, birds, reptiles and amphibians and 3,000 varieties of vegetation. The Company has a long-term agreement for the exclusive global theme park rights to build AVATAR-themed lands and plans to open Pandora - The World of AVATAR at Disney's Animal Kingdom in 2017.

- ***Hotels and Other Resort Facilities*** — As of October 3, 2015, the Company owned and operated 18 resort hotels at the Walt Disney World Resort, with a total of approximately 23,000 rooms and 3,000 vacation club units. Resort facilities include 468,000 square feet of conference meeting space and Disney's Fort Wilderness camping and recreational area, which offers approximately 800 campsites.

- ***Retail*** -- The Walt Disney World Resort also hosts a 127-acre retail, dining and entertainment complex, Disney Springs (formerly Downtown Disney). Disney Springs is home to Cirque du Soleil, the House of Blues and the World of Disney retail store, which features Disney-branded merchandise. A number of the Disney Springs facilities are operated by third parties that pay rent to the Company. Disney Springs is undergoing an expansion that is expected to be completed in 2016.

- ***Other Hotels*** -- Nine independently-operated hotels with approximately 6,000 rooms are situated on property leased from the Company.

- ***ESPN Wide World of Sports Complex*** – This is a 230-acre sports center that hosts professional caliber training and competitions, festival and tournament events and interactive sports activities. The complex, which welcomes both amateur and professional athletes, accommodates multiple sporting events, including baseball, basketball, football, soccer, softball, tennis and track and field. Its stadium, which has a seating capacity of approximately 9,500, is the current spring training site for MLB's Atlanta Braves.

- ***Other*** -- Other recreational amenities and activities available at the Walt Disney World Resort include three championship golf courses, miniature golf courses, full-service spas, tennis, sailing, water skiing, swimming, horseback riding and a number of other noncompetitive sports and leisure time activities. The resort also includes two water parks: Disney's Blizzard Beach and Disney's Typhoon Lagoon.

## Disneyland Resort

The Company owns 486 acres and has the rights under long-term lease for use of an additional 55 acres of land in Anaheim, California. The Disneyland Resort includes two theme parks (Disneyland and Disney California Adventure), three hotels and Downtown Disney, a retail, dining and entertainment complex.

- **Disneyland** — Disneyland consists of eight themed areas: Adventureland, Critter Country, Fantasyland, Frontierland, Main Street USA, Mickey's Toontown, New Orleans Square and Tomorrowland. These areas feature themed attractions, shows, restaurants, merchandise shops and refreshment stands. Additionally, Disneyland offers daily parades, a nighttime fireworks extravaganza and a nighttime entertainment spectacular, *Fantasmic!*. In August 2015, the Company announced it will be constructing a new Star Wars-themed land at Disneyland.
- **Disney California Adventure** — Disney California Adventure is adjacent to Disneyland and includes seven themed areas: Buena Vista Street, Cars Land, Grizzly Peak, Hollywood Land, Pacific Wharf, Paradise Pier and "a bug's land". These areas include attractions, shows, restaurants, merchandise shops and refreshment stands. Additionally, Disney California Adventure offers a nighttime water spectacular, *World of Color*.
- **Hotels and Other Resort Facilities** — Disneyland Resort includes three Company-owned and operated hotels with a total of approximately 2,400 rooms, 50 vacation club units and 180,000 square feet of conference meeting space.
- *Downtown Disney*-- This a themed 15-acre outdoor complex of entertainment, dining and shopping venues, is located adjacent to both Disneyland and Disney California Adventure. A number of the Downtown Disney facilities are operated by third parties that pay rent to the Company.

## Aulani, a Disney Resort & Spa

Aulani, a Disney Resort & Spa, is a Company operated family resort on a 21-acre oceanfront property on Oahu, Hawaii featuring 351 hotel rooms, an 18,000-square-foot spa and 12,000 square feet of conference meeting space. The resort also has 481 Disney Vacation Club units.

## Disneyland Paris

The Company has an 81% effective ownership interest in Disneyland Paris (see recapitalization discussion below), a 5,510-acre development located in Marne-la-Vallée, approximately 20 miles east of Paris, France, which has been developed pursuant to a master agreement with French governmental authorities. The Company manages and has a 77% equity interest in Euro Disney S.C.A., a publicly-traded French entity that is the holding company for Euro Disney Associés S.C.A., the primary operating company of Disneyland Paris. The Company also has a direct 18% ownership interest in Euro Disney Associés

S.C.A. Disneyland Paris includes two theme parks (Disneyland Park and Walt Disney Studios Park); seven themed hotels; two convention centers; a shopping, dining and entertainment complex (Disney Village); and a 27-hole golf facility. Of the 5,510 acres comprising the site, approximately half have been developed to date, including the Val d'Europe development discussed below. An indirect, wholly-owned subsidiary of the Company is responsible for managing Disneyland Paris. Euro Disney Associés S.C.A. is required to pay royalties and management fees to the Company based on the operating performance of the resort.

- **Disneyland Park** — Disneyland Park consists of five themed areas: Adventureland, Discoveryland, Fantasyland, Frontierland and Main Street USA. These areas include themed attractions, shows, restaurants, merchandise shops and refreshment stands. Disneyland Park also features a daily parade and a nighttime entertainment spectacular, *Disney Dreams!*.

- **Walt Disney Studios Park** — Walt Disney Studios Park takes guests into the worlds of cinema, animation and television and includes four themed areas: Backlot, Front Lot, Production Courtyard and Toon Studio. These areas each include themed attractions, shows, restaurants, merchandise shops and refreshment stands.
- **Hotels and Other Facilities** — Disneyland Paris operates seven resort hotels, with approximately 5,800 rooms and 210,000 square feet of conference meeting space. In addition, several on-site hotels that are owned and operated by third parties provide approximately 2,300 rooms.
- Disney Village is a 500,000-square-foot retail, dining and entertainment complex located between the theme parks and the hotels. A number of the Disney Village facilities are operated by third parties that pay rent to a subsidiary of Euro Disney S.C.A.
- Val d'Europe is a planned community near Disneyland Paris that is being developed in phases. Val d'Europe currently includes a regional train station, hotels and a town center consisting of a shopping center as well as office, commercial and residential space. Third parties operate these developments on land leased or purchased from Euro Disney S.C.A. and its subsidiaries.

## Hong Kong Disneyland Resort

The Company owns a 47% interest in Hong Kong Disneyland Resort through Hongkong International Theme Parks Limited, an entity in which the Government of the Hong Kong Special Administrative Region (HKSAR) owns a 53% majority interest. The resort is located on 310 acres on Lantau Island and is in close proximity to the Hong Kong International Airport. Hong Kong Disneyland Resort includes one theme park and two themed hotels. A separate Hong Kong subsidiary of the Company is responsible for managing Hong Kong Disneyland Resort. The Company is entitled to receive royalties and management fees based on the operating performance of Hong Kong Disneyland Resort.

- Hong Kong Disneyland — Hong Kong Disneyland consists of seven themed areas: Adventureland, Fantasyland, Grizzly Gulch, Main Street USA, Mystic Point, Tomorrowland and Toy Story Land. These areas feature themed attractions, shows, restaurants, merchandise shops and refreshment stands. Additionally, there are daily parades and a nighttime fireworks extravaganza, *Disney in the Stars*. A new themed area based on Marvel's Iron Man franchise is under construction and expected to open in late 2016.
- Hotels — Hong Kong Disneyland Resort includes two themed hotels with a total of 1,000 rooms. A third hotel with 750 rooms is under construction and expected to open in 2017. (See Note 6 to the Consolidated Financial Statements for more information on hotel financing.)

## Shanghai Disney Resort

The Company and Shanghai Shendi (Group) Co., Ltd (Shendi) are constructing a Disney resort (Shanghai Disney Resort) in the Pudong district of Shanghai, which will be located on approximately 1,000 acres and will initially include the Shanghai Disneyland theme park; two themed hotels with a total of 1,220 rooms; a retail, dining and entertainment complex; and an outdoor recreational area. Construction on the project began in April 2011, with the resort opening date planned for spring 2016. The total investment will be funded in accordance with each shareholder's equity ownership percentage, with approximately 67% from equity contributions and 33% from shareholder loans. Shanghai Disney Resort is owned

21

through two joint venture companies, in which Shendi owns 57% and the Company owns 43%. A management company, in which the Company has a 70% interest and Shendi a 30% interest, is responsible for designing, constructing and operating Shanghai Disney Resort. The management company will be entitled to receive management fees based on operating performance of the resort. The Company is also entitled to royalties based on resort revenues.

## Tokyo Disney Resort

Tokyo Disney Resort is located on 494 acres of land, six miles east of downtown Tokyo, Japan. The resort includes two theme parks (Tokyo Disneyland and Tokyo DisneySea); three Disney-branded hotels; six independently operated hotels; Ikspiari, a retail, dining and entertainment complex; and Bon Voyage, a Disney-themed merchandise location.

**Tokyo Disneyland** — Tokyo Disneyland consists of seven themed areas: Adventureland, Critter Country, Fantasyland, Tomorrowland, Toontown, Westernland and World Bazaar.

**Tokyo DisneySea** — Tokyo DisneySea, adjacent to Tokyo Disneyland, is divided into seven "ports of call," including American Waterfront, Arabian Coast, Lost River Delta, Mediterranean Harbor, Mermaid Lagoon, Mysterious Island and Port Discovery.

**Hotels and Other Resort Facilities** — The resort includes three Disney-branded hotels with a total of more than 1,700 rooms and a monorail, which links the theme parks and resort hotels with Ikspiari.

## Disney Vacation Club

Disney Vacation Club (DVC) offers ownership interests in 13 resort facilities located at the Walt Disney World Resort; Disneyland Resort; Vero Beach, Florida; Hilton Head Island, South Carolina; and Oahu, Hawaii. Available units at each facility are offered for sale under a vacation ownership plan and are operated as hotel rooms when not occupied by vacation club members. The Company's vacation club units consist of a mix of units ranging from deluxe studios to three-bedroom grand villas. Unit counts in this document are presented in terms of two-bedroom equivalents. DVC had 3,807 vacation club units as of October 3, 2015. In September 2015, the Company announced that its next planned vacation project will be at Disney's Wilderness Lodge at the Walt Disney World Resort.

## Disney Cruise Line

Disney Cruise Line (DCL) is a four-ship vacation cruise line, which operates out of ports in North America and Europe. The *Disney Magic* and the *Disney Wonder* are 85,000-ton 877-stateroom ships, and the *Disney Dream* and the *Disney Fantasy* are 130,000-ton 1,250-stateroom ships. DCL caters to families, children, teenagers and adults, with distinctly-themed areas and activities for each group. Many cruise vacations include a visit to Disney's Castaway Cay, a 1,000-acre private Bahamian island.

22

# Chapter 2
# The Defining Technology

In all product platforms, one element or layer stands above all others, defining the real nature of that platform. It defines the platform's capabilities and limitations. It is critical to understanding the platform and defines the unique characteristics of all products developed from the platform. In successful product platforms, this layer is unique and provides a sustainable vector differentiation for competitive advantage. The lifecycle of the platform is usually dependent on the continuing strength of this layer or element. This is why this critical platform layer or element is referred to as the Defining Technology.

A couple of important characteristics of the defining technology are worth noting. The lifecycle of the platform is usually dependent on defining technology's continuing strength. When the defining technology begins to be replaced by another better competitive technology, the success of the platform, and all of its products, begins to decline. This is the unique vulnerability of a product platform strategy that we will discuss later. We will examine this when we discuss platform lifecycle management.

Competitive advantage is usually derived from the defining technology. It creates the primary vector of differentiation (unique theme) for all products, and it's strategically important to continuously improve your defining technology. If you can keep making major improvements, you create an increasingly larger competitive advantage. When competitors catch up or copy your defining technology then your vector of differentiation narrows. That's why its best described as a vector. Major improvements to your defining technology create a steep vector. Diminishing improvements flatten the vector and give competitors a chance to catch up. This is one of the characteristics defining a robust platform strategy that we will discuss later.

The defining technology has several important characteristics:

- It's important to give a priority to investing in and continually enhance your defining technology
- Successful defining technologies will almost certainly be copied by competitors
- Patent protection is a big advantage (examples: new drugs, K-Cups)
- In absence of patent protection, it becomes more important to continually stay ahead of competition by improving your defining technology
- At some point, competitors may match your defining technology and you need to compete on other factors
- Never get lulled into thinking that your reputation is your competitive advantage

23

- Markets and competitive positions in a market can be characterized by understanding the differences, or lack of differences, in defining technologies
- Rapid evolution of defining technology enables new derivative platforms at much lower price points to serve larger markets
- Defining technology is also the key to creating derivative platforms that enable expansion into new markets.

The best way to illustrate defining technology is through actual examples.

## DEFINING TECHNOLOGY EXAMPLES

A product platform provides strategic focus and focusing on defining technology enables you to focus on what's most important. Otherwise product strategy devolves into an endless stream of product features. Let's look at some examples.

### APPLE'S DEFINING TECHNOLOGY

In the Apple platform, the iOS software is the defining technology. It provided the first real touch-based handheld computer in the iPhone. Along with functions like manipulation, multi-touch gestures, and rotations in the initial versions, it created a unique product. Apple has continued to improve this platform layer with new capabilities added every year.

| Software iOS | | | | | | | | | | |
|---|---|---|---|---|---|---|---|---|---|---|
| User Interface | Direct Manipulation | Multi-Touch Gestures | Rotation | Wi-Fi | Cellular | Home Screen | Folders | Notification Center | Multi Tasking | Utilities | Siri |

When it was first released, Apple's defining technology was unique. It has since been copied, but Apple invests heavily into improving it in order to stay ahead of its primary competitor, Android. When Steve Jobs began planning the iPhone, he had a choice to either "shrink the Mac, which would be an epic feat of engineering, or enlarge the iPod". Jobs decided on the former approach The decision enabled the success of the iPhone as a platform for third-party developers: using a well-known desktop operating system as its basis allowed the many third-party Mac developers to write software for the iPhone with minimal retraining.

The operating system was unveiled with the iPhone at the Macworld Conference & Expo, January 9, 2007, and released in June of that year. At first, Apple marketing literature did not specify a separate name for the operating system, stating simply what Steve Jobs claimed: "iPhone runs OS X" and runs "desktop applications" when in fact it runs a variant of [Mac] OS X.

On September 5, 2007, Apple released the iPod Touch, which had most of the non-phone capabilities of the iPhone. Apple also sold more than one million iPhones during the 2007 holiday season. On January 27, 2010, Apple announced the iPad, featuring a larger screen than the iPhone and iPod Touch, and designed for web browsing, media consumption, and reading iBooks.

24

In June 2010, Apple rebranded iPhone OS as "iOS". Apple is currently releasing iOS 10 in September of 2016.

## AMAZON'S DEFINING TECHNOLOGY

Amazon's defining technology has evolved to be combination of its two layers for finding and evaluating products. It has built an amazing library of reference information with ratings to help customers choose the right products. It also introduced many critical platform technologies, such as its one-click buying.

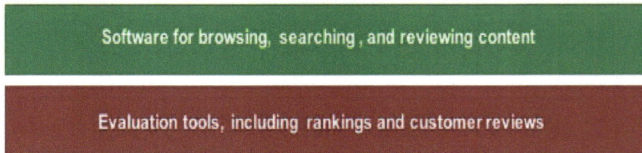

Amazon pioneered ecommerce technology for search for a product or browsing categories of products. Amazon allows users to submit reviews to the web page of each product. Reviewers must rate the product on a rating scale from one to five stars. Customers may comment or vote on the reviews, indicating whether they found a review helpful to them. If a review is given enough "helpful" hits, it appears on the front page of the product. In 2010, Amazon was reported as being the largest single source of Internet consumer reviews. The Amazon sales rank (ASR) provides an indication of the popularity of a product sold on any Amazon locale. It is a relative indicator of popularity that is updated hourly. Effectively, it is a "best sellers list" for the millions of products stocked by Amazon. 1-Click buying is the technique of allowing customers to make online purchases with a single click, with the payment information needed to complete the purchase having been entered by the user previously. This enables the customer to purchase an item without having to use shopping cart software. The United States Patent and Trademark issued a patent for this technique to Amazon in 1999. Amazon also owns the "1-Click" trademark

Amazon has tried to patent other parts of its defining technology as well. Here are just a few of Amazon's dozens of patents:

- Internet-based customer referral system, U.S. Patent 6,029,141, February 22, 2000
- Content personalization based on actions performed during a current browsing session, U.S. Patent 6,853,982, February 8, 2005
- Method and system for integrating transaction mechanisms over multiple internet sites, U.S. Patent 6,882,981, April 19, 2005
- Use of product viewing histories of users to identify related products, U.S. Patent 6,912,505, June 28, 2005

## KURIG'S DEFINING TECHNOLOGY

Kurig's defining technology is easy, its patented K-cup brewing technology. The company's flagship products, Keurig K-Cup brewing systems, are designed to brew a single cup of coffee, tea, hot chocolate,

25

or other hot beverage. The grounds are in a single-serve coffee container, called a "K-Cup" pod, consisting of a plastic cup, aluminum lid, and filter. Each K-Cup pod is filled with coffee grounds, tea leaves, cocoa powder, fruit powder, or other contents, and is nitrogen flushed, sealed for freshness, and impermeable to oxygen, light, and moisture.

The machines brew the K-Cup beverage by piercing the foil seal with a spray nozzle, while piercing the bottom of the plastic pod with a discharge nozzle. Grounds contained inside the K-Cup pod are in a paper filter. Hot water is forced under pressure through the K-Cup pod, passing through the grounds and through the filter. A brewing temperature of 192 °F (89 °C) is the default setting, with some models permitting users to adjust the temperature downward by five degrees. The key original patent on the K-Cup expired in 2012.

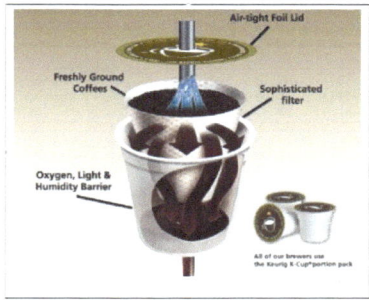

In 2015, Kurig introduced an entirely new platform, the Kurig Kold, for single serving cold beverages, such as Coke who they have a partnership with. This platform did not use Kurig's defining technology at all, and wasn't able to leverage its advantages. The new platform failed because it was too bulky, too expensive, it was loud and unreliable, and drinks were much more expensive than bottled drinks. Kuring recalled the new platform from the market nine months after it was introduced. The failure of the Kurig Kold illustrates the increased risk of a company expanding into new markets without leveraging its defining technology.

## NATIONAL INSTRUMENTS DEFINING TECHNOLOGY

National Instruments defining technology is its LabVIEW software. This is comprehensive software that enables many instruments to be connected to a common platform and provides the measure necessary for each instrument. As was discussed, this was a very different approach to individual instrumentation products.

## ALARM.COM'S DEFINING TECHNOLOGY

The defining technology at Alarm.com is its cloud-based shared multi-tenant software platform that enables multiple services to millions of customers through a broad array of devices.

## TESLA'S DEFINING TECHNOLOGY

Tesla's defining technology is built upon its unique drive train particularly its battery technology and the elements such as the cells, inverter, motor and gear box that work together as a system. Unlike other automakers, Tesla does not use single-purpose, large battery cells, but thousands of small, cylindrical, lithium-ion commodity cells used in laptops and other consumer electronics devices. It uses a version of these cells that is designed to be cheaper to manufacture and lighter than standard cells by removing some safety features. According to Tesla, these features are redundant because of the advanced thermal management system and a intumescent chemical in the battery to prevent fires. Panasonic, a Tesla Motors investor, is the only supplier of the battery cells for the car company.

Tesla Motors may have the lowest costs for electric car batteries, estimated at US$200 per kWh. This defining technology also enables Tesla vehicles to travel 200 plus miles between charges, a very big advantage over other electronic vehicles. Tesla's defining technology incorporates many elements that are patented and others that are proprietary.

## PIXAR'S DEFINING TECHNOLOGY

The Pixar defining technology is based on its digital animation technology, such as RenderMan image processing technology and all of its continuing upgrades. This enables it to produce exceptionally high-quality animated films in a highly efficient way. Its most prominent use of technology is software which allows them to create the animation in their films. Pixar also relies on powerful, specially designed computers to use for the process of rendering.

RenderMan, now the industry-standard software for rendering (the process of generating finished two-dimensional images from the geometry, surfacing and lighting data used to create a three-dimensional animation)was first used (after some pilot films) to create Toy Story. 2001's Monsters, Inc. used the on-screen representation of fur.

Finding Nemo pioneered new techniques in digital lighting, which were used to create realistic-looking water. The Incredibles and Ratatouille applied advances in the simulation of crowds and fluids. Up used advances demonstrated simulation of balloons and feathers. 2012's Brave applied an algorithm which produced realistic vegetation and forestry; and Monsters University re-designed the way lighting and shadow is used at the studio. Pixar is constantly innovating the way they use technology, and improving its defining technology.

## WANG LABORATORIES FAILURE TO UNDERSTAND ITS DEFINING TECHNOLOGY

It sometimes can be difficult to understand the defining technology, and not understanding the defining technology will frequently lead to failure. Wang Laboratories is a clear case of a company that failed to understand its defining technology. In the late 1970s, Wang established a dominant position in word-processing systems: most large companies were using Wang word-processing systems to increase their typing productivity. With the arrival of the PC, however, special-purpose word-processing equipment became too limited and too expensive. Wang failed to apply this new technology because it didn't understand that the defining technology its word processing platform was its software, not its hardware. What if Wang had understood its defining technology and converted its word-processing software to run on IBM and Apple PC? Most likely it would have become the dominant word processing application software company since it was already the standard that most people use. Perhaps today Wang would be a large software company, as successful as Microsoft.

Why did Wang make this fatal mistake? It wasn't because the executives were stupid or didn't understand technology. Quite the contrary was true. It was simply a matter of not understanding what technology was really the defining technology. The obvious technology is not always the defining technology.

# Chapter 3
# Product-Line Strategy

Product-line strategy is a time-phased conditional plan for the sequence of developing products from a common platform. There are several important elements in this definition. A product-line strategy determines the sequence in which products are developed and released. This sequence is time phased throughout the lifecycle of the platform and product line. Finally it is conditional in that it can change with evolving market conditions, competitive factors, or resource availability.

With a platform strategy, each new product leverages the underlying platform and new products can be deployed much faster. This enables more products to better serve multiple market segments while also providing greater consistency of products though a common platform. Finally, leveraging a common platform enables much shorter product lifecycles in a product-line strategy.

## INGREDIENTS OF A PRODUCT-LINE STRATEGY

A platform strategy enables the rapid and efficient release of many new products, but a poorly implemented product-line strategy can restrict the success of a product-platform strategy. A company can miss opportunities to target distinct market segments, or confuse the market with a proliferation of products. There are several ingredients to a successful product-line strategy.

1. *The platform enables frequent release of multiple products.* The nature of product-platform leverage means that new products can be created with less investment in R&D by simply adding new capabilities or changes to fit new market segments.
2. *The product-line covers all primary targeted market segments.* Various product offerings within a product line are intended to appeal to different types of customers. Collectively, the products within a product line should cover the major segments of the market. Sometimes this is done by adding new capabilities for market segments not currently served. Other times it is done varying product features within different price ranges.
3. *Each product offering is sufficiently focused to avoid product proliferation and market confusion.* In order to appeal to everyone, some companies have a tendency to create too many products, especially because this is easier within a platform strategy. This product proliferation can be tempting, but it also can cause confusion among customers in choosing products, as well as creating supply-chain inefficiencies.

29

4. *Individual products are frequently grouped within product families.* A product family is a set of very similar products aimed at a market segment, and generally has several price points and features within the family.
5. *There also may be a product-line strategy to encourage up-selling within the product line.* In some cases, one element of the strategy is to get customers interested at a low price point, but then get them to upgrade to higher price point products.
6. *The product-line development schedule is time phased.* Generally, a company can't release all products in a product line at the same time, so the release schedule is important. Typically, the release schedule will focus initially on the primary market segments, and then progressively broaden target markets through lower and higher prices and increased features.

## PRODUCT-LINE STRATEGY EXAMPLE: THE APPLE IPAD PRODUCT LINE

Let's look at the Apple iPad as a product-line example, illustrated below. With the September 2015 announcement of the new iPad Pro, Apple reconfigured its iPad product-line strategy. It has three iPad product families: the iPad mini, the iPad Air, and the iPad Pro. Each of these families is targeted at distinct market segments.

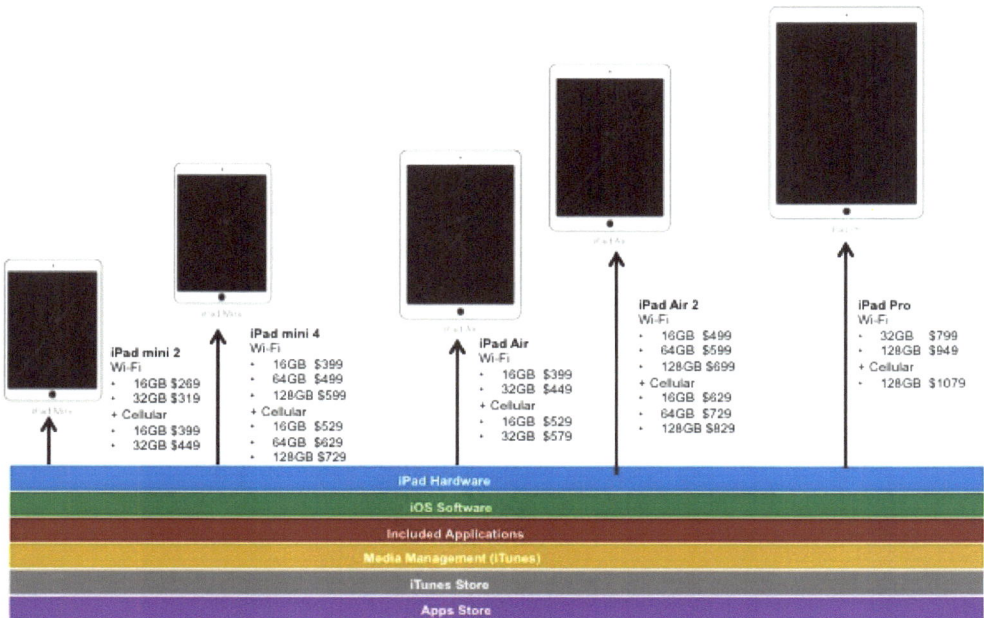

The iPad mini is targeted at the low-end of the market using two products with several variations. At $269 the iPad mini 2 is the low-price entry point, targeted at the entry-level price-conscious user who may be new to the iPad and sees only limited use. For example, this user could be someone who expects to be a casual user who may use it for email and reading books. The iPad mini 2 has a small 7.9" display as its primary segmenting characteristic, and comes in four variations: Wi-Fi with 16GB and 32GB, and Wi-Fi with cellular in 16GB and 32GB. It is the second-generation iPad mini, originally released in 2013. It has an older A7 processor and some other limited capabilities.

Apple's product-line strategy is to introduce new advanced models every year while retaining a previous generation, but reduce the price to keep expanding the lower end of the market. When the iPad mini was originally introduced the lowest price was $329, but it has since been reduced to $269. Apple also discontinued the highest price version of the iPad mini when the iPad mini 4 was introduced to clarify the focus on the low end of the market.

The iPad mini 4 has the same smaller screen size but has more advanced technology and performance. It has the faster second-generation A8 processor, which is much faster. It includes the fingerprint identity sensor, and many other additional features. This model is targeted at the same low-end, limited-use market, but it is intended to upgrade the target user to a better product.

The iPad Air was first introduced in 2013 with an entirely new display from the previous iPad. Apple continued to sell the iPad at a lower price until it introduced the iPad Air 2 in 2014 with touch ID. At that time, it discontinued the previous generation iPad, lowering the price of the previous iPad Air by $100 to cover the lower-priced segment of the full iPad market. It also discontinued the 128MB version of the iPad Air, moving customers who needed more capacity to the 128MB version of the iPad Air 2 instead.

In September 2015, Apple introduced an entirely new product line, the iPad Pro aimed primarily at the business market segment. It has a much larger display with 12.9" compared to 9.7" for the iPad Air, and it is much more powerful with the third-generation A9X processor. It also introduced the Apple Pencil as an accessory for the iPad Pro. The iPad Pro pricing is much higher than the iPad Air: $799 for 32GB with just Wi-Fi up to $1,079 for the 128GB with cellular. At the same time, Apple also introduced new multitasking software capabilities with split screen functions that make the most of the larger iPad. This new product is expected to better penetrate the business market segment. Apple's strategy for waiting until now to create the iPad Pro was driven by the time it took for the necessary technologies to become affordable.

In March 2016, Apple introduced the new 9.7 inch iPad Pro, an extension to the original iPad Pro. In doing this, Apple also repositioned the iPad Air 2 as the full size entry point, replacing the iPad Air. It reduced the price of the iPad Air 2 by $100, replacing the price point occupied by the iPad Air.

In addition to the iPad products illustrated in the chart, there are also a number of product variations. The iPad comes in three different colors and the versions with cellular capabilities for hundreds of country and carrier-specific variations.

Let's summarize Apple's iPad product line strategy:

1. It entered the market with its first product in 2010 aimed at the center of the market, getting the most coverage possible.

2. It introduced the smaller iPad mini two years later in 2012 addressing the lower end of the market
3. It then introduced the larger iPad Pro in 2015 addressing higher end of the market.
4. Six months later, it expended the iPad Pro family with a smaller 9.7 inch version, and then re-positioned the iPad Air 2 into the slot previously occupied by the iPad Air.
5. Apple's product line strategy is to refresh its products every year.
6. At that time, it generally continues selling the product it introduced the previous year, but lowers the price, usually by $100.
7. It also retires the product it introduced two years earlier, selling only two different models at one time.

## APPLE IPHONE UPDATE CYCLES

The Apple iPhone also illustrates a regular product line tempo to product upgrades. What is sometimes called linked "S" curves or the Tick-Tock cycle is illustrated in the chart. Essentially this is a two-year upgrade cycle with a major upgrade in the even numbered years (iPhone 3G, 4, 5, 6) and minor upgrades in the odd years (iPhone 3GS, 4s, 5s, 6s). Alternatively, the Tick years are major upgrades, followed by the Tock years for minor upgrades.

Form factors, particularly size, are typically changed in the major update (Tick) years. The iPhone 5 introduced a larger screen, and the iPhone 6 and 6 Plus introduced larger screens and a larger iPhone version.

This cadence allows the company to structure its product development, typically working on two new models in parallel. Then picking

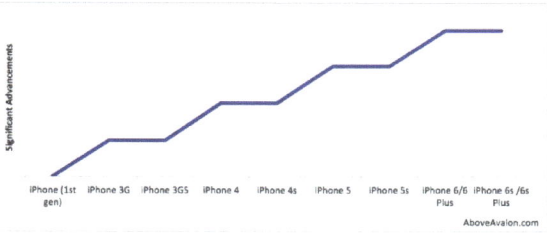

and choosing which features will be released on what new phone. The intermediate iPhone 5s introduced Touch ID, which was a major new feature, but not a form-factor change. The intermediate 6s introduced 3D touch another major feature, which involved a new screen but not a new form factor. This implies that Apple's product-line strategy revolves more around the changing form factors every other year than the value of the upgrade

## AMAZON'S PRODUCT-LINE STRATEGY

Amazon created its success on an amazing product-line strategy built on a common platform by consistently deploying products from its online retail platform as "stores" or product categories. Even when Amazon launched its online bookstore in 1995, its vision wasn't limited to books. Amazon's vision was to be the "Everything Store".

32

In 1998, it launched the music store and the DVD/video store in 1998. This was the first logical new product category extension from books. The next year, it launched eight new product categories from its online retail platform. This included toys& games and home improvement. And then Amazon launched new product categories almost every year, consistently leveraging its online retail platform. In 15 years, this strategy led Amazon to become a $60 billion company.

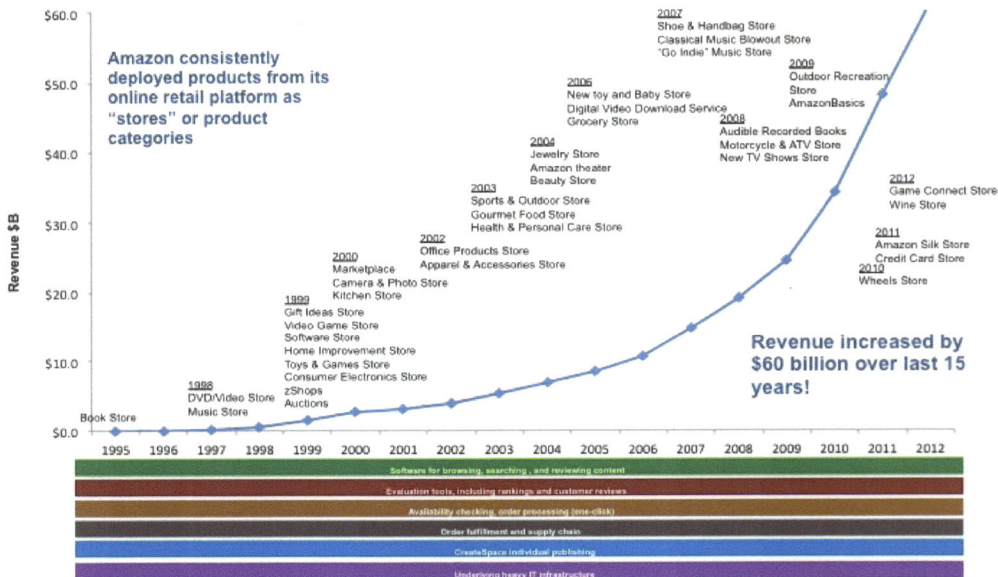

Every improvement Amazon made to its online platform was leveraged across all product categories, and the shear mass of Amazon's product offerings created a competitive advantage, such as "one-stop shopping". Others tried to get into online merchandise sales with individual point-solution category products, but couldn't compete with Amazon's platform and scale advantages. Pets.com did an IPO in 1998 and went out of business in 2000. Its customer acquisition costs were $300 per customer, much higher than Amazon's. eToys was created in 1997 but went out of business in 2001.

33

# Chapter 4
# Continuous Platform Improvement
# (Vector of Differentiation)

Successful companies achieve unique product differentiation primarily through the underlying product platform, not their individual products. The differentiation in a product platform provides the constant theme woven throughout the product-line built on it, with individual products providing variations on that theme. This differentiation is frequently referred to as the vector of differentiation.

Differentiation is a way of distinguishing a product's value from competing products in order to get customers to purchase that product instead of a competitor's.

- *Differentiation positions a product in the market.* Product differentiation combined with price defines the relative positioning of competitive products in a marketplace. For example, one product may have more features or capabilities and justify a higher price. Customers who value these features or capabilities will pay the higher price, those who don't will gravitate to the lower price product.
- *Differentiation segments the market.* Market segmentation has two different meanings. A population or market can be segmented by various customer characteristics. The other meaning of market segmentation is based on the differentiation of competitive products. Relating the two types of segmentation enables a company to effectively target prospective customers.
- *Differentiation evolves throughout a product and market lifecycle.* Differentiation is not static. Competitors will try to emulate favorable differentiation and try to create new differentiation. Continuous improvement, especially at the platform level, is critical.

Because of constant improvement, differentiation is best viewed as a vector not an individual point. A vector provides a path for continuous improvement in a specific direction. A vector of differentiation is not stagnant; it is a direction for continuous improvement.

## IPHONE CONTINUOUS IMPROVEMENT PATH

In a product-platform strategy, continuous platform improvement is critical. This is done from constant attention in adding new elements to the platform layers and improving individual elements, and periodically adding new platform layers. Again using Apple as an example, continuously improves each of the layers in its platform. In the iOS software layer, it annually releases a new software upgrade with new

34

elements and improvements such as Apple Pay, touch ID, and 3D touch. At the same time it also releases new embedded applications and improvements to almost every previous one.

Apple also annually releases new improvements to the iPhone hardware layer as can be seen in the chart illustrating six years of annual improvements. Let's look at the improvement over time in in this layer. The heart of the iPhone, its CPU, was upgraded in 2009 with a faster 600 MHz ARM, then improved again in 2010 to 800 MHz, and in 2011 to a faster dual-core ARM. Then in 2012, Apple made an even bigger improvement with the Apple A6 is a 32-bit package on package (PoP) system on a chip (SoC) designed by Apple. Then in 2013, it was upgraded from a 32-bit processor to a 64-bit, setting the stage for even more capabilities in the future. Improvements to the memory elements went from 128 MB of DRAM in the first generation to 1 GB in the iPhone 5. As can be seen in the chart, continuous improvements also were made in the power, display graphics, camera, sensor and other elements.

| | 1st Gen 6/29/2007 | iPhone 3G 7/11/2008 | iPhone 3GS 6/19/2009 | iPhone 4 6/24/2010 | iPhone 4S 10/14/2011 | iPhone 5 9/29/2012 | iPhone 5c/5s 9/20/2013 |
|---|---|---|---|---|---|---|---|
| CPU | Samsung 32-bit RISC ARM | | 600 MHz ARM Cortex-A8 | 800 MHz ARM Cortex-A8 | 800 MHz dual-core ARM Cortex-A9 | 1.3 GHz dual core Apple A6 | 1.3 GHz dual core Apple A6/A7 (64-bit) |
| Memory (DRAM) | 128 MB LPDDR DRAM (137 MHz) | | 256 MB LPDDR DRAM (200 MHz) | 512 MB LPDDR2 DRAM (200 MHz) | 512 MB LPDDR2 DRAM | 1 GB LPDDR2 DRAM | 1 GB LPDDR3 DRAM |
| Power | 3.7 V 5.18 W-h (1400 mAh) | 3.7 V 4.12 W-h (1150 mAh) | 3.7 V 4.51 W-h (1219 mAh) | 3.7 V 5.25 W-h (1420 mAh) | 3.7 V 5.3 W-h (1432 mAh) | 3.8 V 5.45 W-h (1440 mAh) | 3.8 V 5.92 W-h (1560 mAh) |
| System on a chip | | | | Apple A4 | Apple A5 | Apple A6 | Apple A7 (5c) |
| Display | 3.5 in 3:2 aspect ratio, scratch-resistant glossy glass covered screen, 262,144-color (18-bit) TN LCD, 480×320 px (HVGA) at 163 ppi, 200:1 contrast ratio | | Added a fingerprint-resistant oleophobic coating and 262,144-color (18-bit) TN LCD with hardware spatial dithering | Retina display 3.5 in (89 mm), 3:2 aspect ratio, aluminosilicate glass covered 16,777,216-color (24-bit) IPS LCD screen, 960×640 px at 326 ppi, 800:1 contrast | | 4.0 in (100 mm);16:9 aspect ratio;1136 x 640 px screen resolution at 326 ppi | |
| Graphics | PowerVR MBX Lite 3D GPU[11] (103 MHz) | | PowerVR SGX535 GPU (150 MHz) | PowerVR SGX535 GPU(200 MHz) | PowerVR SGX543MP2 (2-core) GPU | PowerVR SGX543MP3 (3-core) GPU | |
| Cellular Connectivity | Quad band GSM/GPRS/EDGE (850, 900, 1,800, 1,900 MHz) | 3G cellular and A-GPS location. Tri-band 3.6 Mbps UMTS/HSDPA (850, 1,900, 2,100 MHz) | Added 7.2 Mbit/s HSDPA | 4G | 14.4 Mbit/s HSDPA (4G on AT&T) Dynamically switching dual antenna.[263] Combined GSM/CDMA World phone ability | LTE, HSPA+ and DC-HSDPA | |
| Camera | Fixed-focus 2.0-megapixel camera on the back for digital photos | | 3.2-megapixel camera with autofocus, auto white balance, and auto macro. Also capture 640×480 video at 30 frames per second | VGA front-facing camera for video calling and a 5-megapixel rear-facing camera with 720p video capture | Dynamically switching dual antenna.[263] | Panorama using the built-in camera app. and also can take still photos while recording video | 5s - updated camera with a larger aperture and dual-LED flash; 5s - backside-illuminated FaceTime camera |
| Sensors | Proximity Sensor Ambient Light Sensor Accelerometer | | Added Magnetometer | Added Gyroscopic Sensor | | | |
| Sim Card | Mini-SIM | | | Micro-SIM | | Nano-SIM | |
| Dimensions | 115 mm (4.5 in) H 61 mm (2.4 in) W 11.6 mm (0.46 in) D | 115.5 mm (4.55 in) H 62.1 mm (2.44 in) W 12.3 mm (0.48 in) D | | 115.2 mm (4.54 in) H 58.6 mm (2.31 in) W 9.3 mm (0.37 in) D | | 123.8 mm (4.87 in) H 58.6 mm (2.31 in) W 7.6 mm (0.30 in) D | |

## NEW GENERATION PLATFORM IMPROVEMENT STRATEGY

Another way to consistently improve product platforms is to create a new and improved platform for subsequent generations. Tesla Motors' first production vehicle, the Tesla Roadster, was an all-electric sports car. The Roadster was the first highway-capable all-electric vehicle in serial production for sale in the United States in the modern era. The Roadster was also the first production automobile to use lithium-ion battery cells and first mass production battery electric vehicle to travel more than 200 miles (320 km) per charge.

Tesla's product roadmap has always consisted of three vehicle platforms. The first was the Roadster, although those were built by hand so there wasn't an actual manufacturing platform. The second includes

Model S and Model X, and Model 3 will be built on the third-generation platform. After Model 3 will come Model Y, also built on the same third-generation platform. Each subsequent platform incorporates advances in many areas, but particularly battery technology where the cost curve aggressively lowers battery costs.

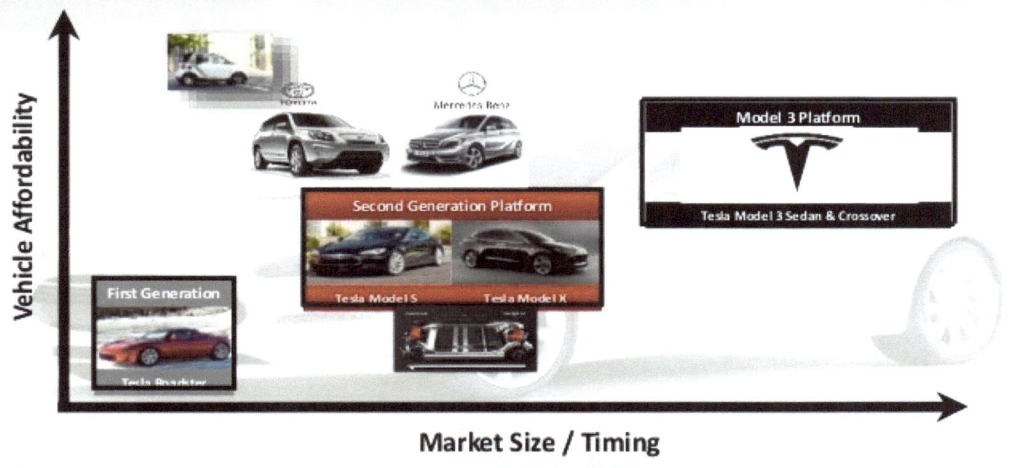

## Product Roadmap – Growing EV Volume

Vehicle Affordability

First Generation
Tesla Roadster

Second Generation Platform
Tesla Model S    Tesla Model X

Model 3 Platform
Tesla Model 3 Sedan & Crossover

Market Size / Timing

# Chapter 5
# Platform Ecosystems

One of the things we've learned over the years about platform strategy is that it does not exist in isolation. Others can also create products and services from your platform, so you need to look at a platform more broadly as a "Platform Ecosystem." This may include applications that run on your platform, products that supplement your platform, content that runs on your platform, and indirect sales channels that sell your platform, service organizations that support your platform, and even competitive products that may use your platform in some way.

The figure illustrates a typical platform ecosystem with your platform in the middle. Below your platform are partners and suppliers of key components, materials, subsystems and possibly software. Above your platform are others who provide services, content, and applications, as well as dealers, resellers, etc., who sell the product. In some cases, solution partners or providers may provide invaluable value to your platform in specific customer situations. In fact, your platform may be dependent on the products of another. It could be an imbedded component in other platforms.

A platform ecosystem strategy is about control. Strategically you need to identify which parts of your platform "revenue portfolio" you want to control and which ones you are willing to let others control. The best way to look at this is to understand the total revenue pie from the entire ecosystem.

- *Revenue leakage* occurs when others generate revenue from your platform that you could derive and would like to have.
- *Revenue imbalance* occurs when others get more revenue for the value they provide, and you get a smaller piece of the pie than you deserve for the value you provide.
- *Platform partnership* occurs when there is a strategic balance and interdependence. In some cases, these partners are fulfilling functions that you don't want to or are unable to do.
- *Platform control* is defined by who has control of the broader platform ecosystem. It always best to be in control and not have the success of your platform dependent on others.
- *Irrelevant revenue* by others occurs when you don't care at all about another's revenue stream

Strategically, as part of your platform strategy, you want to map out this ecosystem and try to estimate the total revenue for everything in the platform ecosystem. Then look at who has what power in the broader platform ecosystem. Are there new strategies you could be following to improve you position and increase you revenue in this platform ecosystem?

## INTEL'S PLATFORM ECOSYSTEM STRATEGY

Intel follows a successful platform strategy for its microprocessors. My 2000 book on Product Strategy illustrated this with a successful example of the 486 product-line deployed over time addressing multiple market segments from a common platform. But Intel microprocessors are part of a broader platform ecosystem; in fact they are generally at the bottom of the ecosystem. During the 1990s, Intel addressed this with a new ecosystem strategy.

First in 1991, it launched the popular: "Intel Inside" marketing and branding campaign. The idea of ingredient branding was relatively new at the time with only NutraSweet and a few others making attempts to do so. This campaign established Intel, which had been a component supplier little-known outside the PC industry, as more of a household name. It also used this campaign to reinforce that the Intel component was essential and not easily replaced by a competitor's microprocessor, because at the lowest level of the broader platform infrastructure, Intel was more vulnerable.

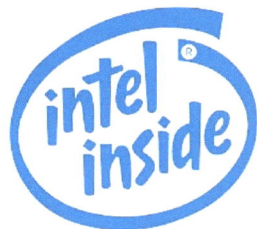

The second strategy was lesser known. Intel's Systems Group began, in the early 1990s, manufacturing PC "motherboards", the main board component of a personal computer, and the one into which the microprocessor and memory (RAM) chips are plugged. Shortly after, Intel began manufacturing fully configured "white box" systems for the dozens of PC clone companies that rapidly sprang up. At its peak in the mid-1990s, Intel manufactured over 15% of all PCs, making it the third-largest supplier at the time. During the 1990s, Intel's Architecture Lab was responsible for many of the hardware innovations of the personal computer, including the PCI Bus, the PCI Express bus, and the Universal Serial Bus (USB). IAL's software efforts met with less success; its video and graphics software was important in the development of software digital video, but later its efforts were largely overshadowed by competition from Microsoft.

## KEURIG'S PLATFORM ECOSYSTEM STRATEGY

Keurig Green Mountain revolutionized home coffee brewing with its K-Cup machines, essentially creating the single-serve home market in the United States. Keurig Green Mountain has steadily grown K-Cup sales from 1.94 billion units in 2009 to nearly 12 billion in 2014. Keurig's platform ecosystem strategy focused on the sale of K-Cups. Sometimes called the razor-blade strategy, most of the profit is made from the subsequent purchase of the consumable associated with the product. Keurig managed to get tens of millions of Americans to psy per cup for the coffee they brew in their own kitchens, and as long as its patents lasted, it was the only company that could sell the single-serve pods their Keurig coffee machines. But when those patents expired a big part of that lucrative arrangement came to an end. Other companies could now produce their own versions of the so-called K-cup, and advertise them as being compatible with Keurig machines, without paying a royalty to Keurig.

Keurig lost control over the most critical part of its platform ecosystem. Actually it began to lose control over that part of its platform ecosystem earlier when thousands of Keurig single-serve machine fans found a cheaper alternative: refillable, non-disposable K-cups, little plastic coffee grounds holders, which the company sold under the brand of My K-Cup. Not only was it cheaper, but the coffee drinker had more choice, as My K-Cup could be filled with any brand of coffee off the shelf.

In order to regain the revenue from that critical part of its platform ecosystem, in August 2014, Keurig introduced the 2.0 line of coffeemakers, and it stopped making My K-Cup for it. The machine was incompatible with any K-cups already in existence, as well as with any unlicensed disposable K-cups made by other companies. It looked like a brilliant platform ecosystem strategy, but it backfired. Sales of Keurig machines tanked, and they began to accumulate on the shelves across the country. Sales of brewers and accessories declined by 23 percent, and its stock price fell. Finally Keurig capitulated. "We heard loud and clear from consumers," said CEO Brian Kelley, "who really wanted the My K-Cup back. We want consumers to be able to use any brand and bringing the My Cup back allows that." Frequently controlling the platform ecosystem is very difficult.

## SAP'S PLATFORM ECOSYSTEM STRATEGY

SAP is one of the most successful enterprise software companies in the world, and it has a robust platform infrastructure of partners. Implementation consultants are one part of the broader platform infrastructure. SAP has approximately 15,000 implementation consultants, but other partners in the platform ecosystem provide most of the implementation services with approximately 200,000 implementation consultants. This represents approximately $50 billion in revenue for other firms as part of the broader SAP platform

39

infrastructure. There are varied reasons why SAP accepts this in its platform ecosystem strategy: (1) they don't have the skill set to manage consulting services at a larger scale, (2) they prefer to focus on software and not services, and (3) they hope to increase sales by having these other consultants partner with them in promoting SAP software.

## APPLE'S PLATFORM ECOSYSTEM STRATEGY

Here again Apple provides another textbook example of controlling a platform ecosystem strategy. As illustrated, Apple has exerted tight control over its platform ecosystem, creating large and profitable profit streams from major portions of this ecosystem.

Apple introduced the initial layers of the iOS platform with iTunes and then the iPod. Its first move to control and expand its ecosystem was in content with the iTunes store in April 2003. Apple convinced the music companies to sell individual songs for $0.99 with Apple keeping $0.30 of each sale. Apple progressively added content in movies, TV shows, newspapers and magazines. Later, in September 2006, Apple introduced a platform derivative, Apple TV, which leveraged this content revenue stream even more broadly.

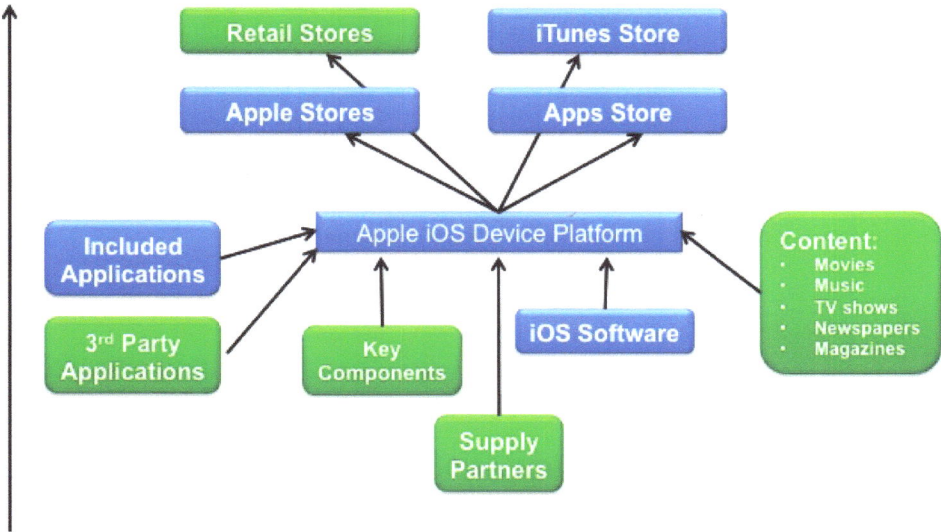

In July 2008, Apple launched the App Store, enabling third parties to develop and sell apps for the iPhone and subsequently the iPad and Apple Watch. And in 2015, Apple introduced the new Apple TV. While it now seems like an obvious move, at the time it was controversial. When the iPhone first came out in early 2007 there were no apps, other than those included by Apple. Steve Jobs argued against allowing any, but was persuaded that eventually others would find a way to do it. Apple then constructed a well-crafted process for testing, authorizing and selling independent apps through its new App Store. Apple was able to control this critical part of its ecosystem and generate significant revenue. Apps billings in 2014 were almost $15 billion with independent developers receiving approximately $10 billion of this.

Overall iTunes, App Store and services revenue was approximately $18 billion in 2014, and about 11% of Apples revenue. If this were a separate company, it would be one of the larger Fortune 500 companies. Clearly, Apple's platform ecosystem strategy has been very successful.

Apple's control over the platform ecosystem extended into retail sales. In May 2001, Apple decided to open its first Apple Store. Here again, this was a controversial decision to control part of its platform ecosystem. Apple's retail store revenue exceeds $20 billion, making it one of the largest retailers in the world, with the highest sales per square foot. The retail stores are also strategic in that they enable Apple to control the release of new products. Enabling customers to get a fitting and try out the new Apple Watch is an example of this.

Apple also extends its ecosystem control into the design of critical components. The Apple "Ax" series is a family of Systems on a Chip (SoC) used in the iPhone, iPad, iPod Touch, and Apple TV. They integrate one or more ARM-based processing cores (CPU), a graphics processing unit (GPU), cache memory and other electronics necessary to provide mobile computing functions within a single physical package. They are designed by Apple, and manufactured by contract manufacturers such as Samsung. The A8X SoC used in the iPad Air 2 uses a 20 nm process with a triple-core CPU running at 1.5 GHz and an 8-core GPU, while the A4 SoC in the first generation iPad used a die manufactured on a 45 nm process with a single-core CPU running at up to 1 GHz. The A9X SoC was used to power the higher performance necessary on the new iPad Pro. It also uses the 64-bit architecture, but it is 2.5 times faster than the A7 processing power and 5X faster for graphics processing.

Apple clearly has a vertically integrated platform ecosystem strategy of controlling all of the critical elements of the broader ecosystem platform, from processor design to retail sales.

# Chapter 6
# Derivative Platforms vs. Alternative Platforms

Derivative Platforms leverage much of the existing platform, usually the defining technologies, to create a new platform. Typically this new derivative platform will enable the company to expand into a new market, or at least better serve segments of the current market. This ability to leverage platform technologies is one of the critical characteristics of a robust product-platform strategy.

Over the years, there has been some confusion between an alternative platform serving the same broad market and derivative platforms. There are several critical differences. A derivative platform uses much of the technology and elements of the platform it comes from, specifically the defining technology, while an alternative platform may use some of the previous platform elements, it's significantly different. An alternative platform also tends to serve much of the same market, even though it may serve some segments better. An example is a lower-cost platform serving the lower-price segments better.

## ALTERNATIVE PLATFORMS

In general, you want to avoid or at least minimize having multiple alternative platforms serve the same market. Multiple alternative platforms can retard development and hinder competitiveness. One data communication company, for example had two different network-management systems: one based on powerful server technology and another based on a lower-cost PC. The two platforms used different network management software, significantly delaying new software releases, as well as taking longer to update its systems with new communications devices. It would have been much better to try to serve the lower-price segments with the same platform, reducing some functionality and hardware features such as speed and capacity.

In addition to eroding economies of scale, alternative-overlapping platforms can confuse customers. IBM fell into this trap in midrange computing when it had five separate and incompatible platforms: the System/3 platform for small business, The System/38 and System/36 platform, the 8100 platform for distributed processing, the Series/1 platform for transaction processing, and the 4300 platform for running mainframe software on a minicomputer. Customers became confused and frustrated as IBM salespeople contradicted one another, stating that their IBM solution was the best. Eventually IBM realized that it needed to merge these platforms into a single platform and launched the Fort Knox project – one new midrange platform compatible with and replacing the other five.

42

## APPLE'S DERIVATIVE PLATFORMS

Apple also provides an excellent example of creating derivative platforms. From a common platform with the layers we discussed previously (Software iOS, Included Applications, Media Management, Content, and Apps Store), Apple creates four derivative platforms. The iPod touch uses mush of the platform layers implemented in a focused way.

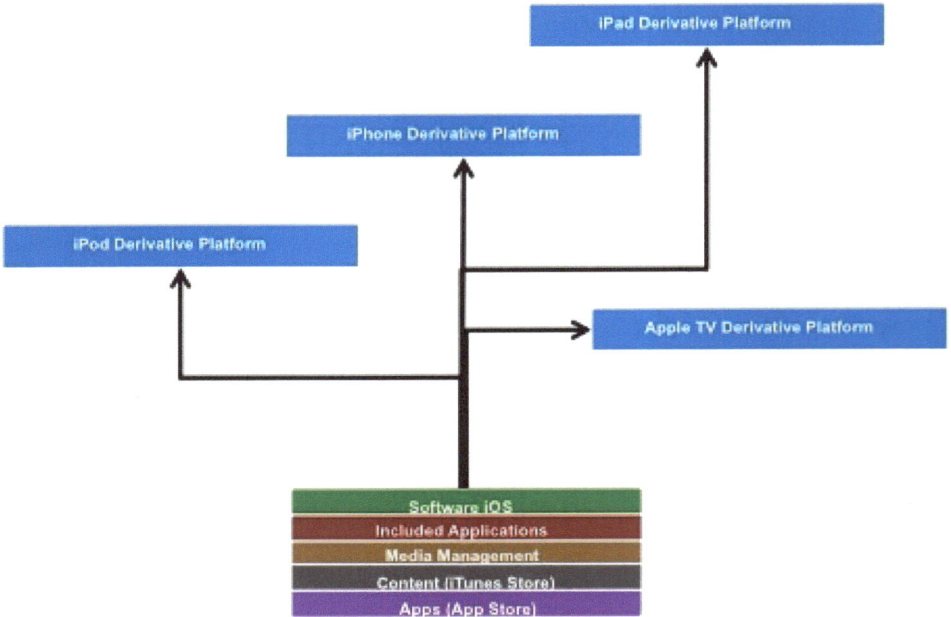

This is different than the original iPad. The iPhone derivative is at the center with the most volume and functionality, using all the platform layers and most elements. The iPad derivative leverages much of the platform that was developed with the iPhone. And finally Apple TV introduced in September 2015 uses many of the platform layers, which is different from the earlier versions of Apple TV.

# Chapter 7
# Leveraged Platform Growth Strategies
# (Highways to Growth)

While every company desires to grow more rapidly, not every company is able to achieve that. Sustained rapid growth almost always comes from continuous deliberate commitment to expansion into new markets. While growth can come from riding rapid market growth with a single product (Google) or from geographical expansion of a single product into new regions or counties (Netflix), the focus here is on growth opportunities to leverage a strong platform into new types of products to penetrate or even create new markets. I believe this provides exceptional sustained growth.

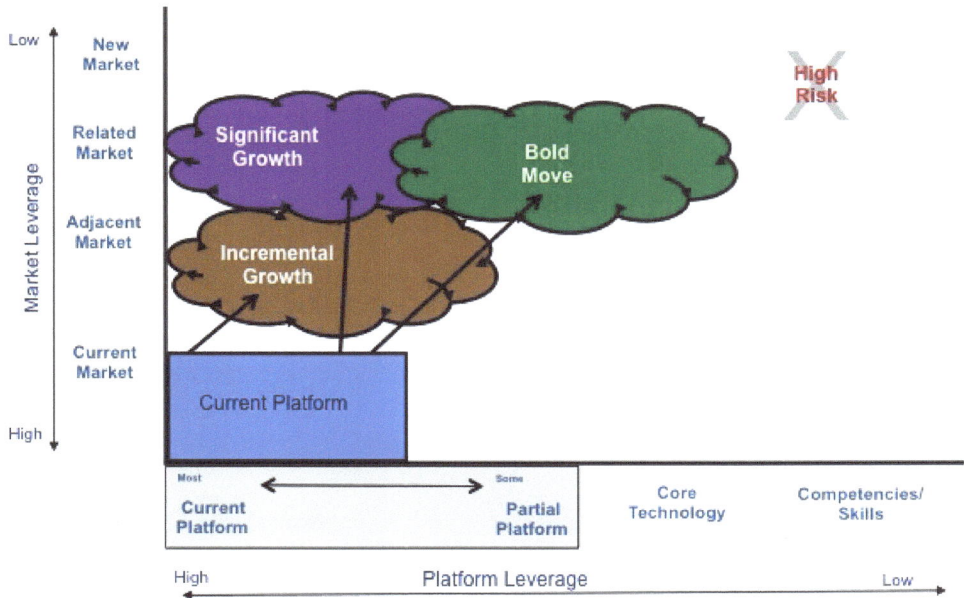

The framework above provides a structure for deliberately identifying new growth opportunities, shows how risk and opportunity varies in each direction, and enables systematic strategic assessment of growth opportunities. Without either the explicit or implicit use of this framework, investments in growth opportunities tends to become haphazard and risky. Many of Google's hundreds of unrelated expansion investments illustrate this approach.

This framework is explained in more detail with many examples in the book *Rapid Growth Through Platform Expansion*, but the following is a summary. Platform leverage follows a spectrum from high by using all or most of the current platform to lower by using little or none. The horizontal axis measures the degree of platform leverage, starting with the current product platform. This provides the highest leverage, but there is varying leverage from use of most of the platform to a partial platform. Continuing on this spectrum is the core technology used in the platform to simply skills and competencies.

Market leverage follows a spectrum from high in the current market served to low in very different markets. On the vertical axis is the the degree of market leverage, starting with the current market. The next step upward is adjacent markets, which are new markets that have characteristics similar to the current market. Then up to new markets that tend to be very different from customers in the current market.

Let's look briefly at the primary expansion paths this provides (others are described in *Rapid Growth Through Platform Leverage*):

**Incremental growth through product-line expansion**. This is expansion into new market segments by adding new products to the current platform. Most significant revenue increases come from serving new market not previously served because incremental revenue from better serving segments already served may not create sufficient growth. The advantages to this type of expansion is lower risk and lower investment. The disadvantages can be that incremental revenue comes from cannibalization of existing products. The Apple iPad Pro is a great example of a current platform modified to better address a new but related market, business users. Amazon's rapid addition of new online stores is another good example.

**Significant growth by creating a derivative platform to expand into a related market**. This is generally a significant growth opportunity because its usually an unserved but related market. This type of market can be large, and emerging related markets are particularly attractive. There is some risk of learning about a new market, but this type of expansion has proven to have the biggest successes. The Apple iPad is an excellent example of this type of expansion, as is National Instruments expansion into embedded monitoring and control with a derivative platform.

**Bold move expansion is expansion into new markets by leveraging only part of the platform and other skills**. These new market can be very attractive, especially new emerging markets with no established competition. The degree of leverage here varies. It can be higher risk as well as higher opportunity. One notable example of success was the original iPhone that leveraged only part of the iPod platform to enter a much bigger market. Other examples include the Amazon Kindle and Microsoft Xbox.

Failure to leverage any of your platform or market experience is extremely risky to the point where failure outnumber successes by 1,000 to 1. Google follows this type of expansion strategy and has had hundreds of failures.

# Chapter 8
# Robust Platform Strategy

An important concept of product platform strategy is platform robustness. A robust product platform enables a company to launch superior products, be more profitable than competitors, and grow rapidly. Many companies have a product platform, and in fact you can say that even a single product is a platform, but many product platforms are weak and limited. To be really successful, you need a robust platform strategy.

## ROBUST PLATFORM STRATEGY CHARACTERISTICS

You can measure the robustness of a product-platform strategy from the following characteristics:

1. *A robust platform generates many products.* The more products built from a common platform, the more robust the platform. A weak or limited platform has only a few products. Consider the Apple platform. It has created many products: all the versions of the iPhone, including new versions every year and versions for all countries; the iPad and its variations, the iPod Touch; the Apple Watch; Apple TV; and revenue-generating services including the App Store, the iTunes store, Apple Pay, Apple Music, etc.
2. *A robust platform has distinct competitive advantages (vectors of differentiation), preferably ones that can be protected from competitors.* Some companies have product platforms that pass the first criteria, but they aren't distinct. For example, IBM's first personal computer launched in August 1981 was a big success. The IBM PC immediately became the market leader and instigated a shake out in the personal computer industry. To get to market faster, however, IBM broke from its tradition and used outside suppliers for the key components. The defining technology of the IBM PC platform was not IBM's. It was based on Intel microprocessors and the Microsoft-developed PC-DOS operating system. While the IBM PC was initially a successful product platform, it did not give IBM sustainable advantage. The vector of differentiation relative to competitors was flat, relying mostly on brand name. PC clone manufacturers were able to quickly acquire the underlying technology and reproduce the platform.
3. *A robust platform is sufficiently complete.* Platforms contain multiple layers and elements, but need to contain all the essential ones in order to be robust. Some platforms are essentially partial and rely on others to complete the platform. Smart phones provide an example. Android software needs to be combined with smart phone hardware from companies such as Samsung to form a complete platform. This limits the ability to combine these two to create new capabilities. Apple,

47

on the other hand, has a complete hardware/software platform for its iPhone, giving it the ability to create new capabilities such as 3D touch that requires both hardware and software innovation.

4. ***A robust platform enables continuous, possibly even rapid, improvement.*** A robust platform gets better and better every year by adding new features, new functionality, and improved performance. Continuously extending the vector of differentiation. It gives customers more reason to buy the products from the platform and makes it difficult for competitors to catch up. In other words, it has a steep vector of differentiation. For example, in iOS 8 Apple made hundreds of improvements to that critical layer of its platform, including photos and camera, notification center, messages, keyboard with Quick Type, family sharing, iCloud, Health Kit, Home Kit, etc. And because it has a robust platform strategy, these improvements were available on almost all iPhones (current, previous, and future) and iPads.

5. ***A robust platform can also spur rapid growth by creating new derivative platforms to expand into new markets.*** As was seen in the previous section, rapid growth can be leveraged by a robust platform. Derivative platforms are based on a common underlying platform, typically the defining technology, and enable a company to grow into new markets. Again looking at Apple as an example, the iPod enabled it to leverage its platform into the iPhone and then the expanded platform was leveraged into the iPad, with Apple TV also using some of the same platform elements.

## TWITTER: EXAMPLE OF A LIMITED PLATFORM

Twitter is an example of a limited platform, one that is not robust. Even though it is referred to as a platform, it is mostly a single product. In fact, Twitter describes itself as a platform: "Twitter, Inc. operates as a global platform for public self-expression and conversation in real time. It offers various products and services for users, including Twitter that allows users to create, distribute, and discover content."

| Twitter Stock Price Decrease | |
|---|---|
| Nov 2013 | $44.90 |
| June 2015 | $35.90 |
| Return | -20% |

However, the Twitter platform is not robust considering the criteria just defined. It really has only a single product, even though it lists a number of other products, these are really just added functionality or different implementations. Promoted tweets, promoted trends, and promoted accounts are its three main sources of revenue, and these are more different markets for the same product. Its platform does not have much proprietary advantage, in fact most of its software is open source and available to others for free. It does make improvements to its platform, but they are usually shared and many are not really significant. It has a relatively flat vector of differentiation. And finally, it has not been able to find new markets opportunities to leverage its platform.

When Twitter came public in November 2013, its stock price soared to $44.90 on the first day, and it even rose to more than $50. Since then, however, it has dropped by 20% in June 2015 to $35.90 per share. Also in June 2015 Twitter fired its CEO.

48

Yahoo provides another example of a company with a limited platform strategy. As can be seen Yahoo has as a relatively thin common platform with minimal leverage. Its primary strategy is a range of individual products, usually content-based web sites, which generate revenue through advertising.

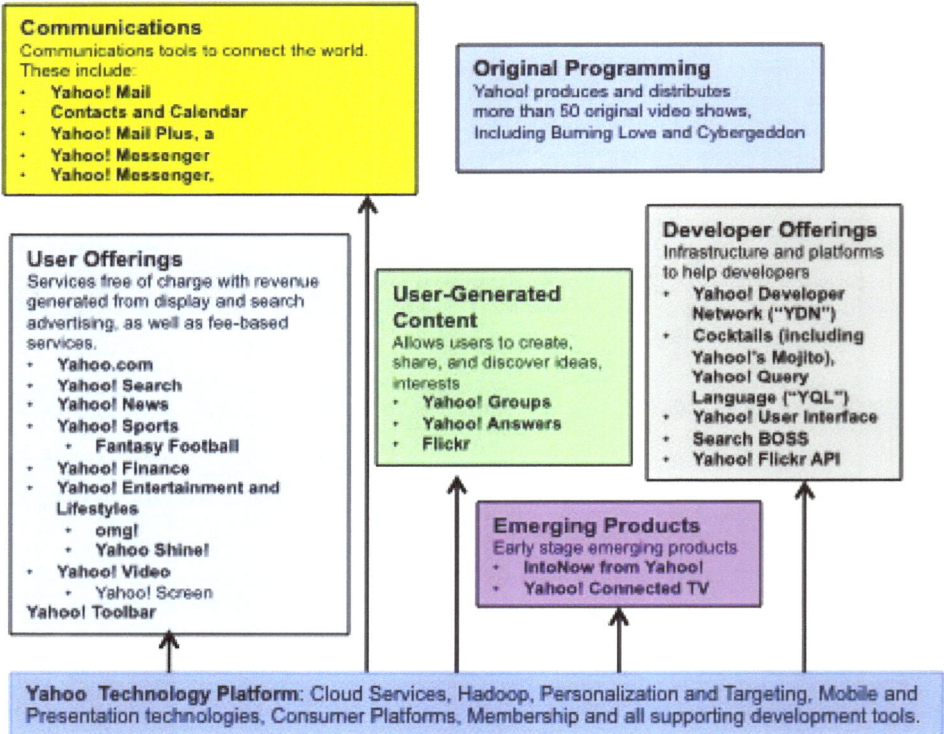

**Communications**
Communications tools to connect the world. These include:
- Yahoo! Mail
- Contacts and Calendar
- Yahoo! Mail Plus, a
- Yahoo! Messenger
- Yahoo! Messenger.

**Original Programming**
Yahoo! produces and distributes more than 50 original video shows, Including Burning Love and Cybergeddon

**User Offerings**
Services free of charge with revenue generated from display and search advertising, as well as fee-based services.
- Yahoo.com
- Yahoo! Search
- Yahoo! News
- Yahoo! Sports
  - Fantasy Football
- Yahoo! Finance
- Yahoo! Entertainment and Lifestyles
  - omg!
  - Yahoo Shine!
- Yahoo! Video
  - Yahoo! Screen
Yahoo! Toolbar

**User-Generated Content**
Allows users to create, share, and discover ideas, interests
- Yahoo! Groups
- Yahoo! Answers
- Flickr

**Developer Offerings**
Infrastructure and platforms to help developers
- Yahoo! Developer Network ("YDN")
- Cocktails (including Yahoo!'s Mojito), Yahoo! Query Language ("YQL")
- Yahoo! User Interface
- Search BOSS
- Yahoo! Flickr API

**Emerging Products**
Early stage emerging products
- IntoNow from Yahoo!
- Yahoo! Connected TV

**Yahoo Technology Platform**: Cloud Services, Hadoop, Personalization and Targeting, Mobile and Presentation technologies, Consumer Platforms, Membership and all supporting development tools.

There is very little leverage of technologies across its products, almost none on a relative basis. This is a relatively high-cost strategy with significant cost to develop and provide current content of each site. In order to deal with its high costs, Yahoo outsourced its search engine product to Microsoft, saving $25M-$30M a month and providing significant upfront payments. Either because of very little platform leverage or because its leadership didn't understand the need for product-platform strategy, Yahoo has had seven CEOs since 2007.

# Chapter 9
# Platform Lifecycles

Understanding the lifecycle of a product platform is the most critical assessment a company must make. It is an irrefutable fact that all product platforms have a lifecycle. Yet most companies seem to ignore this, because they don't think long-term enough. Product lifecycles are much shorter than platform lifecycles. Sometimes there is a regular R&D cadence, such as 1-year or 3-year cycles.

Product platform lifecycles are disruptive. All the products from the platform come to end of life together. This usually implies a very large drop in revenue – frequently fatal, killing companies concentrating on a few platforms. A disruptor's advantage can create new companies that displace old companies. Frequently platform lifecycles end because competitors introduce new technology. It's the frog-in-boiling-water tendency where companies don't recognize the threat until it is too late. There can be a tendency to avoid initiating disruptive change without explicit decision points. Assessment of a platform lifecycle requires a specific strategic process. Most of the time, a decision isn't necessary isn't necessary, but if you don't you can get blind-sided. An annual assessment of product lifecycle is like having an annual physical.

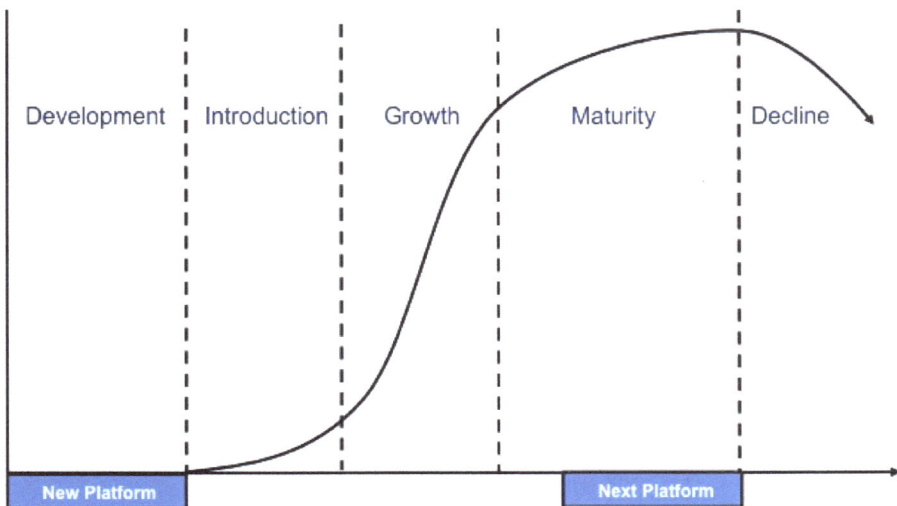

A typical platform lifecycle, as illustrated, starts with the **Development Stage.** A significant investment is needed in the new platform, requiring either a diversion of the R&D portfolio to the new platform or a significant increase in overall R&D investment. It frequently requires new skills and expertise. A link between core strategic vision (CSV) and business model is critical.

During the **Introduction Stage**, the platform is initially launched along with the first products developed from it. The first products are usually aimed at the most attractive market segments, or the safest for initial release, such as early innovators. An intense effort on improving the platform also begins.

In the **Growth Stage** there is usually a big opportunity to release many new products because the incremental development costs for each new product are low and there is usually an opportunity to easily segment and sub-segment the market. The temptation at this point is to launch too many new products, creating product proliferation. At this stage, diminishing returns on new products may be precursor to impending platform maturity.

The **Maturity Stage** is the most critical of all, yet most companies seem to ignore this. Product platform lifecycles are disruptive. All the products from the platform come to end of life together. Usually implies a very large drop in revenue – frequently fatal, particularly companies concentrating on a few primary platforms. Disruptor advantages can create new companies that displace old companies. Frequently platform lifecycles end because competitors introduce new technology. Assessment of platform lifecycle is the most significant strategic judgment, which is needed to trigger development of next-generation platform in time.

## APPLE IPOD LIFECYCLE

Apple's iPod product illustrates a typical product lifecycle, as the iPhone product cannibalized the iPod. The iPod was introduced in October 2001 as a Mac-compatible product that could put 1,000 songs in your pocket. iPod sales rose quickly over the next six years. Some people don't remember that by 2005, Apple sold 20 million iPods, and it was 45% of Apple's revenue.

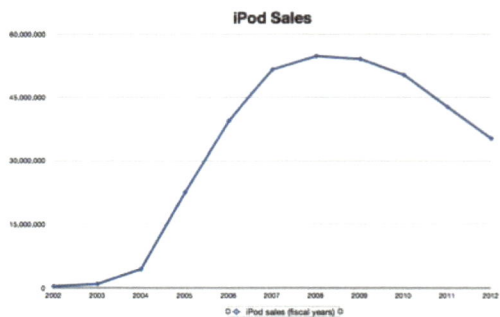

iPod Sales

The iPod was an initial platform that implemented Steve Jobs' Digital Hub Vision. Later Jobs obsessed over what could mess up the iPod success concluding, "The device that could eat our lunch was the cell phone. Everyone carries a cell phone, and that could make an iPod unnecessary." Apple first tried to partner with Motorola on the ROKR, but that was a failure. Then it began to design it's own phone. In the process, it abandoned much of the iPod platform and created a new platform with a multi-touch technology and screen replacing the tack wheel, and new operating software. (Although some of the music and iTunes platform elements were retained.)

51

When the iPhone was introduced in 2007, it began to immediately cannibalize the iPod, as you can see in the chart. By 2012, iPod sales fell by half, but iPhone sales more than replaced this decline.

## THE DEATH OF DIGITAL EQUIPMENT

At its peak in the late 1980s, minicomputer manufacturer Digital Equipment had $14 billion in sales and ranked among the most profitable companies in the world. With its strong staff of engineers, Digital was expected to usher in the age of personal computers, but the autocratic and trend-resistant Mr. Olsen was openly skeptical of the desktop machines, saying "the personal computer will fall flat on its face in business", and regarded them as "toys" used for playing video games.

**Digital Equipment Revenue**

Digital's fortunes declined after missing out on some critical market shifts, particularly toward the personal computer. The board forced Olsen to resign as president in July 1992. On April 15, 1994, Digital reported a loss of $183 million. Sales of the VAX, long the company's biggest moneymaker, continued to decline, which in turn also hurt Digital's lucrative service and maintenance business.

Market's acceptance of Digital Alpha computers and chips had been slower than the company had hoped. Digital eventually made a strong push into personal computers and workstations, which had even lower margins than Alpha computers and chips. Also, Digital played catch-up with its own Unix offerings for client-server networks, as it long emphasized its own VMS software, while corporate computer users based their client-server networks on the industry-standard Unix software (of which Hewlett Packard was one of the market leaders).

Digital's problems were similar to that of larger rival I.B.M., due to the fundamental shift in the computer industry that made it unlikely that Digital could ever again operate profitably at its former size of 120,000 employees, and while its workforce had been reduced to 92,000 people many analysts expected that they would have to cut another 20,000.

Eventually, on 26 January 1998, what remained of the company (including Digital's multivendor global services organization and customer support centers) was sold to PC manufacturer Compaq in what was the largest merger up to that time in the computer industry. At the time of Compaq's acquisition announcement, Digital had a total of 53,500 employees, down from a peak of 130,000 in the 1980s, but it still employed about 65 percent more people than Compaq to produce about half the volume of sales revenues. After the merger closed, Compaq moved aggressively to reduce Digital's high selling, general, and

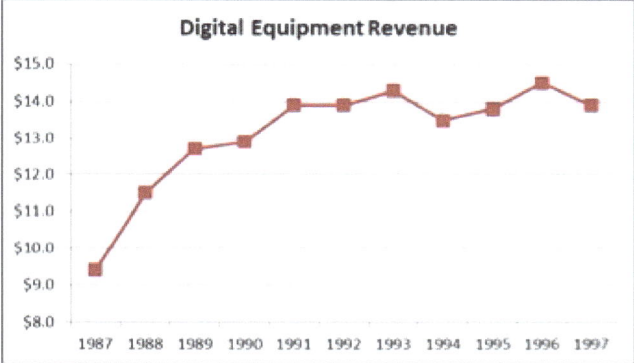

52

administrative (SG&A) costs (equal to 24 percent of total 1997 revenues) and bring them more in line with Compaq's SG&A expense ratio of 12 percent of revenues.

## US RECORDED MUSIC INDUSTRY PLATFORMS

Entire industries also see platform lifecycle declines. This chart shows the dramatic changes in the lifecycle of different music platforms over 30 years. Cassettes and then CDs replaced vinyl and 8-track media. The introduction of CDs also dramatically increased the total market as people spent much more to build collections of CDs. With the advent of digital downloads to portable devices, lead by Apple's innovation of single song sales, music downloads replaced CDs. and the total market declined as people spent less on single tract purchases. Since 2009, an even newer platform, streaming music, has started to replace digital downloads. In 2014, streaming revenue was already $1.3 billion of total music sales compared to $2.5 billion from downloads, and that shift was increasing quickly.

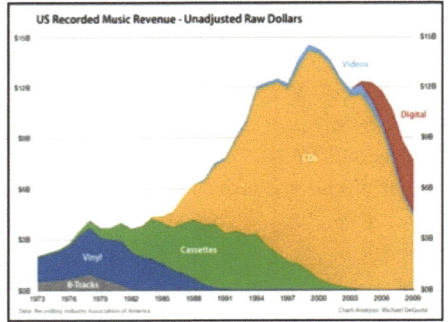

US Recorded Music Revenue - Unadjusted Raw Dollars

## AMEX TRAVELERS CHECK PLATFORM LIFECYCLE

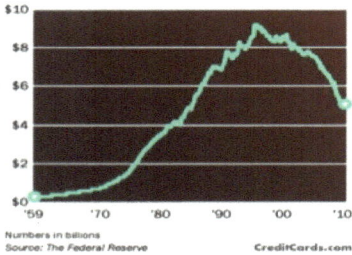

Numbers in billions
Source: The Federal Reserve          CreditCards.com

Even what are perceived as commodity products can have platform lifecycles. In the early 1990s, I gave a strategy presentation to the executives of American Express and discussed the concept of platform lifecycles. I remember them telling me overwhelmingly that Amex traveller Checks were one exception to that rule. I didn't argue the point, but knew they were being myopic. Since then, the volume of Amex Traveller Checks has plummeted as consumers had more alternatives, particularly ATMs. When you could even use your debit or cash card to get cash when you were travelling, even foreign currency while travelling abroad. This diminished the need for Travellers Checks and fewer businesses even accepted them. It's also an example of how a very different technology can threaten a product platform, even one that is not technology based. As can be seen in the chart, the volume of American Express Travelers checks began to drop precipitously around the time that ATMs began to proliferate around the world. Today, many younger people don't even know what a travelers check is, and most retail stores don't even accept them anymore.

53

Netflix provides a great example of a company that introduced a new platform that displaced its competitor and then went on to cannibalize its own platform with an entirely new one. Examples of a company that is astute enough to cannibalize its own platform with a new one are rare.

The idea of Netflix came to Reed Hastings when he was forced to pay $40 in overdue fines by Blockbuster after returning *Apollo 13* well past its due date. Netflix introduced a different platform model built around the monthly subscription concept in September 1999, delivering by US Mail two new DVDs each time the previous one was returned with no limit on the number of movies watched each month, and no late fees. Since that time, the company has built its reputation on the business model of flat-fee unlimited rentals without due dates, late fees, shipping and handling fees, or per title rental fees.

In 2000, Netflix was offered for acquisition to Blockbuster for $50 million; however, Blockbuster declined the offer. At that time Blockbuster was a $5 billion company that collected $800 million per year in late fees alone. Blockbuster had an enormous retail platform of 60,000 employees in 9,000 store locations. But by 2004 Blockbuster peaked, as its platform was undermined by Netflix. Blockbuster's enormous investment in stores blocked its ability to change its platform. From 2002 to 2010, when it declared bankruptcy, Blockbuster lost $4 billion. The new Netflix platform was superior. But the story doesn't end there.

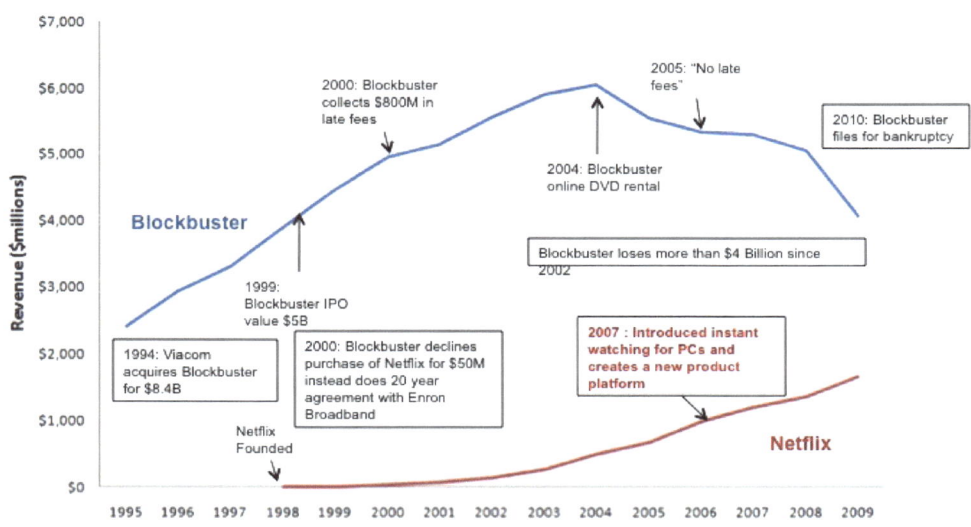

In February 2007, the company delivered its billionth DVD, but began to move away from its original core business model of mailing DVDs. It invested in developing a new technology for video streaming on demand via the Internet. Netflix introduced instant watching for PCs and created a new platform. Its vi-

54

sion was that video streaming on multiple devices would replace DVDs. This required a lot of investment and partnerships to get video devices, such as game devices, in those early days to support streaming over Internet.

This new platform cannibalized its platform at that time, and DVD sales fell from 2006 to 2011, but Netflix recovered from this, growing from $1 billion in 2007 to $2 billion in 2012 and then $5.5 billion in 2014.

# Chapter 10
# Conclusion: The Strategic Leverage of Platform Strategy

Through the concepts and example illustrated here, we have seen the exceptional power of a platform-based strategy:

1. **A platform strategy enables the release of multiple products rapidly, with each of these targeted at specific market segments**. We saw several examples of how a platform strategy enables a company to release many new products quickly from that platform. This can provide an enormous advantage over companies that are still developing point products. National Instruments used this to its advantage in the test and measurement market.

2. **A platform strategy leverages R&D investment across many products**. Because a common product platform, or a set of derivative platforms, is used for multiple products, the R&D investment is highly leveraged. A competitor developing individual products with a unique development cost per product has much higher R&D investment per product than those who leverage a common investment across many products. In addition, a product-platform strategy enables a company to focus its R&D investment on the most critical platform elements, and then use the results in many products.

3. **A platform strategy enables continuous improvement at the platform level that is leveraged across all products from that platform**. Rather than choose which products to invest in, with a platform strategy a company can make continuous improvements at the platform level, and then introduce these across all products from that platform. In the Apple example, investments in new iOS elements are leveraged across all iPhones and iPads.

4. **A platform strategy enables a company to leverage its platform into new market in order to grow rapidly**. We looked at the ways a company can effectively leverage its platform to drive rapid growth by deliberately and continuously expanding into new markets. Apple's expansion from the iPhone to the iPad is a great example.

5. **A platform strategy provides significant product cost leverage**. A common platform also uses common hardware components and shared production. This lowers product material costs because of higher volume procurement and also provides higher manufacturing volume.

6. **A platform strategy also leverages the supply chain**. Similar products can leverage distribution and make the supply chain most efficient, enabling more flexibility of modular products.

7. **A platform strategy can also provide marketing, channel and brand name leverage.** The similarity and defining characteristics of different products from the same product platform makes it easier to market and promote these products.

# Notes:

---

[1] Stock price increase or decrease can be a good metric for the long-term success of a product-platform strategy, although there are obviously other factors involved in stock price increase. The long-term stock price change is used for several examples in this document.

[2] In the 2001 version of my book, Product Strategy, I used amazon as an emerging company with an exceptional long-term platform strategy. When the stock price dropped to less than $8/share I bought quite a bit of stock in the company, although I later sold it for an average price of about $200 per share, deciding not to be greedy.

[3] Stephens Inc. In-Depth report on National Instruments, May 14,2015.

[4] Oppenheimer & Co. Initiation of Coverage: National Instruments Corporation, July 30, 2015.

[5] Fortune Magazine, September 14, 2015

www.ingramcontent.com/pod-product-compliance
Lightning Source LLC
Chambersburg PA
CBHW041720200326
41521CB00001B/136